nickelodeon™

降击神通

AVATAR
THE LAST AIRBENDER™

Created by
Bryan Konietzko
Michael Dante DiMartino

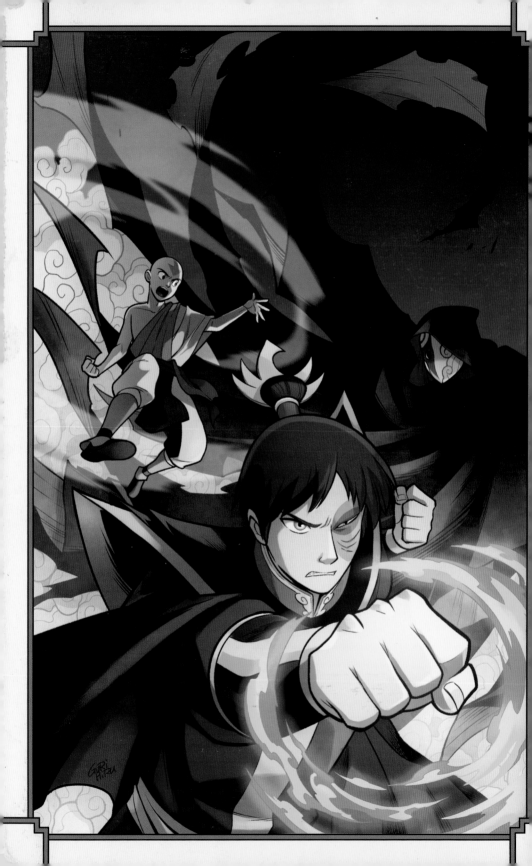

nickelodeon

降击神通

AVATAR

THE LAST AIRBENDER

SMOKE AND SHADOW · PART THREE

script
GENE LUEN YANG

art and cover
GURIHIRU

lettering
MICHAEL HEISLER

DARK HORSE BOOKS

president and publisher
MIKE RICHARDSON

editor
DAVE MARSHALL

assistant editor
RACHEL ROBERTS

collection designer
SARAH TERRY

digital art technician
CHRISTIANNE GOUDREAU

Special thanks to Linda Lee, Kat van Dam, James Salerno, and Joan Hilty
at Nickelodeon, and to Bryan Konietzko and Michael Dante DiMartino.

Published by **Dark Horse Books**
A division of Dark Horse Comics, Inc.
10956 SE Main Street, Milwaukie, OR 97222

DarkHorse.com
Nick.com

International Licensing: (503) 905-2377
Comic Shop Locator Service: (888) 266-4226

First edition: March 2016 | ISBN 978-1-61655-838-3

1 3 5 7 9 10 8 6 4 2
Printed in China

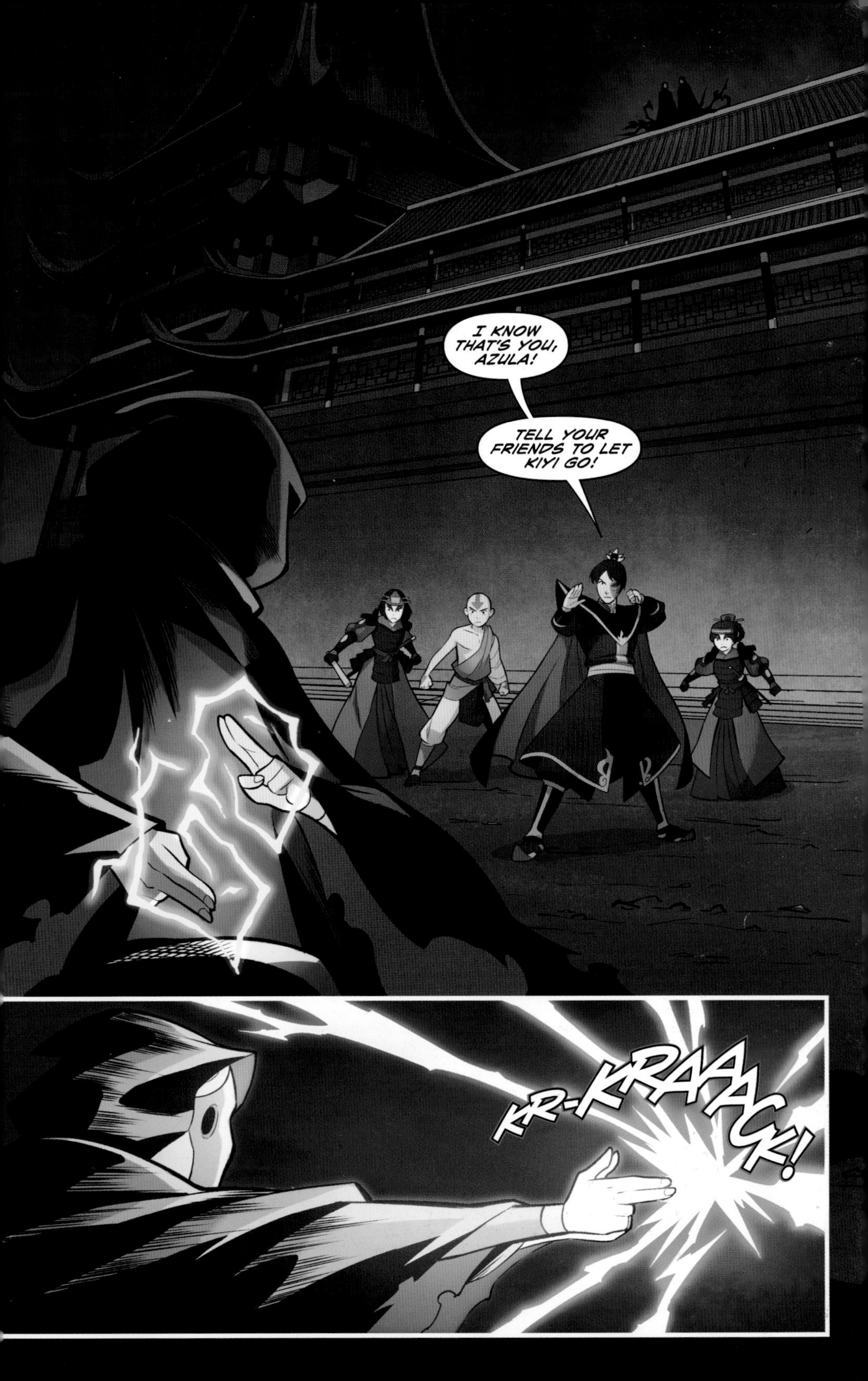
I KNOW THAT'S YOU, AZULA!
TELL YOUR FRIENDS TO LET KIYI GO!
KR-KRAAAACK!

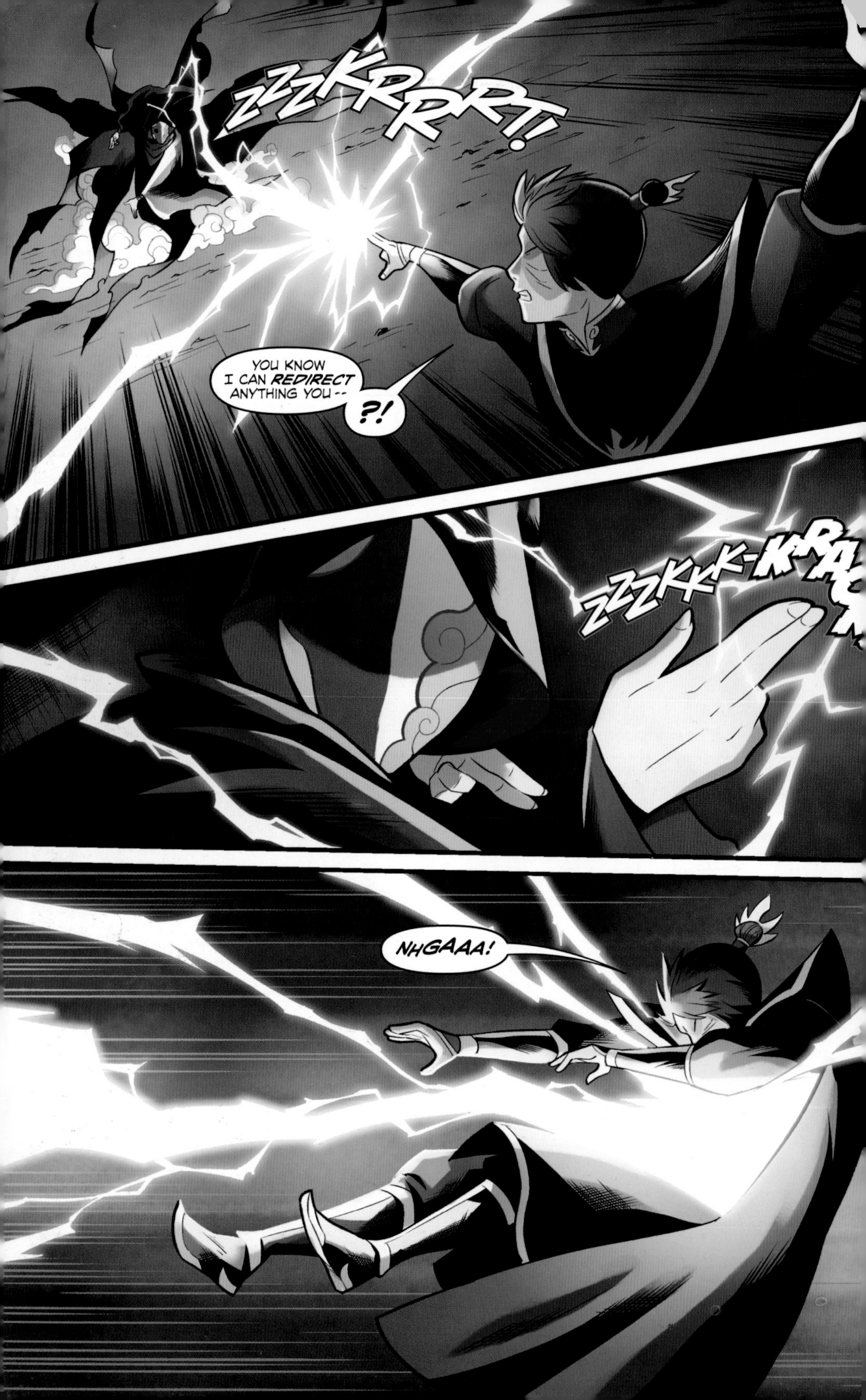
ZZZKRRRT!
YOU KNOW I CAN *REDIRECT* ANYTHING YOU --
?!
ZZZKKK-KRAC
NHGAAA!

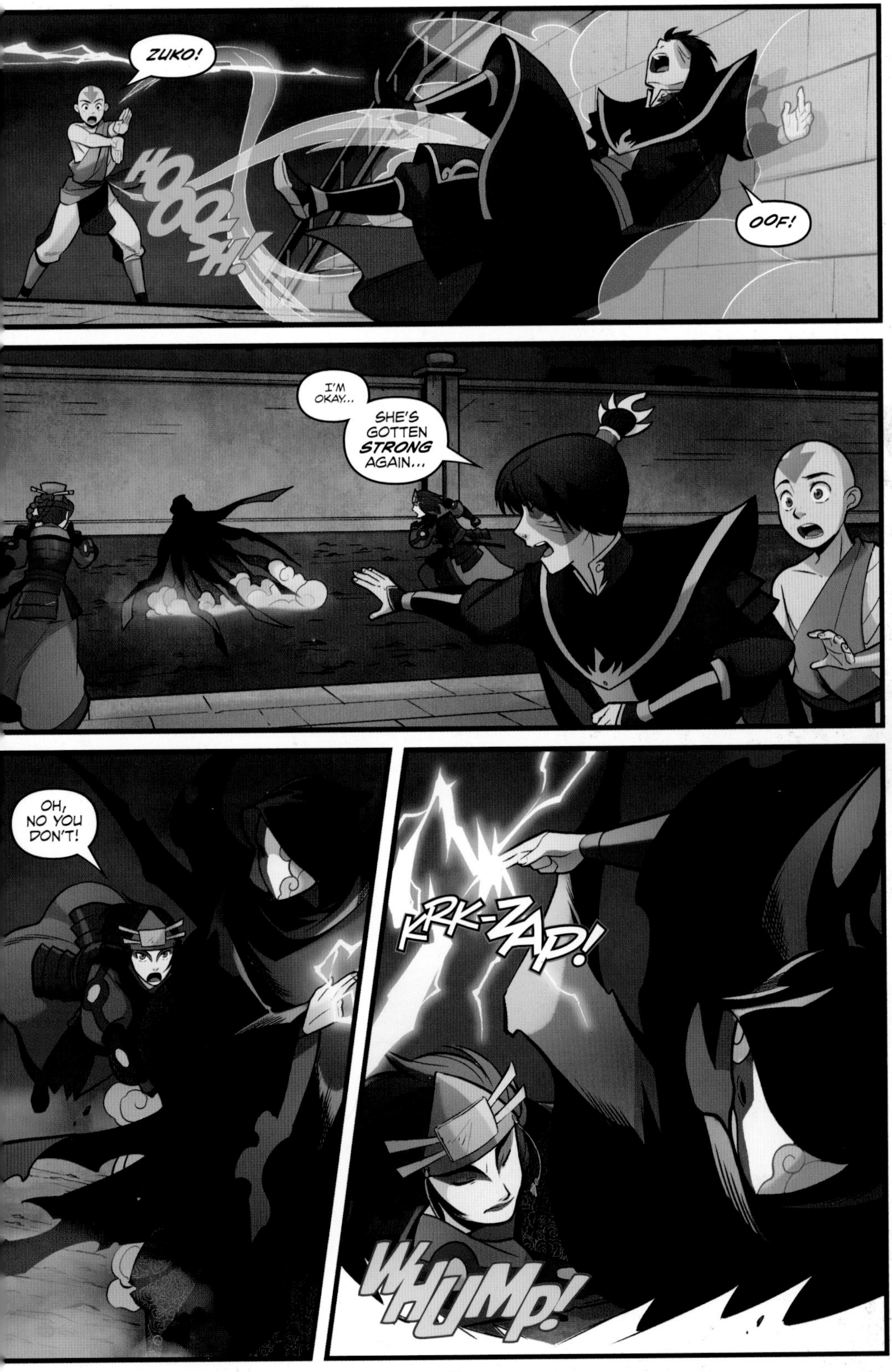
ZUKO!
HOOOSH!
OOF!
I'M OKAY...
SHE'S GOTTEN STRONG AGAIN...
OH, NO YOU DON'T!
KRK-ZAP!
WHUMP!

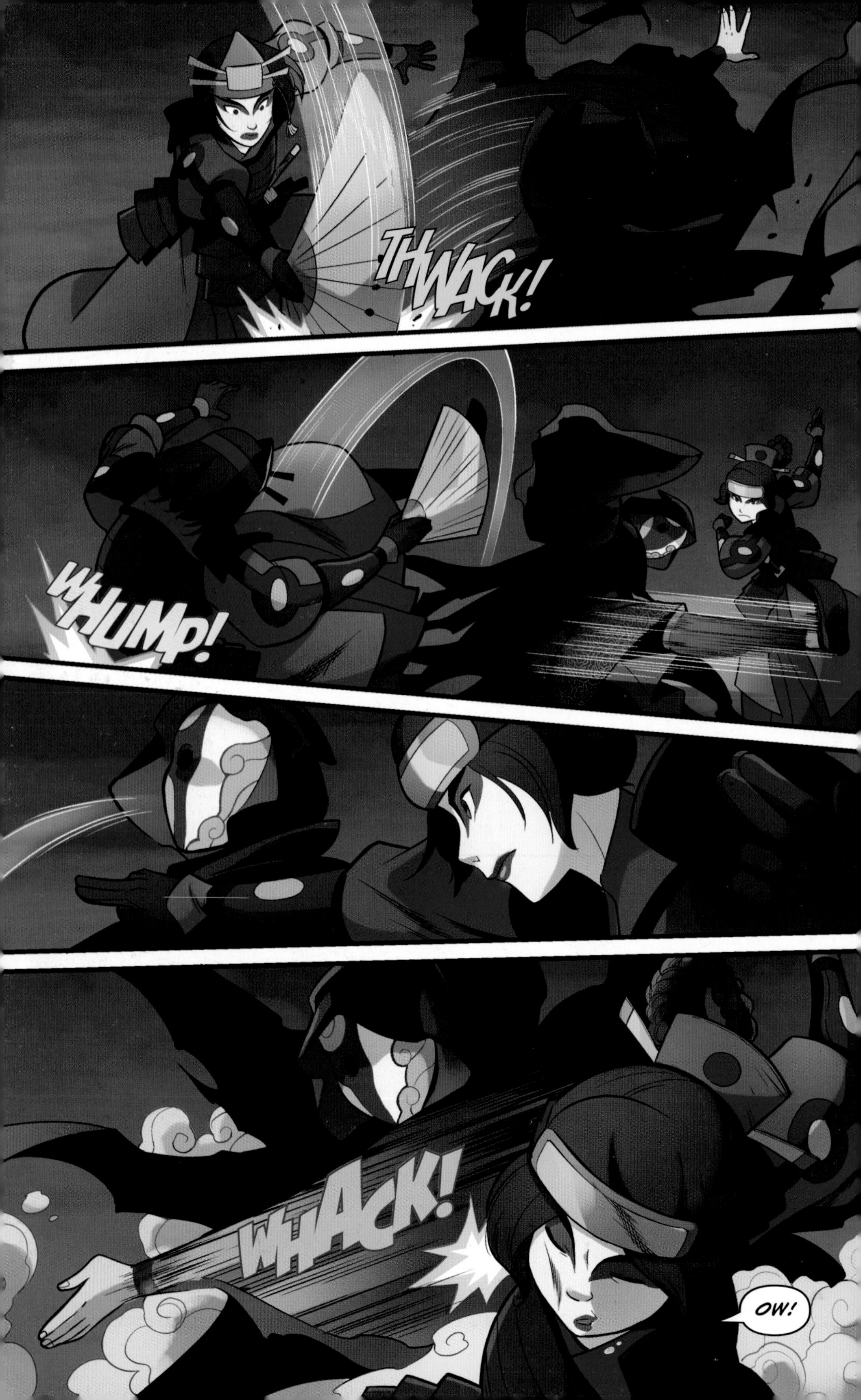
THWACK!
WHUMP!
WHACK!
OW!

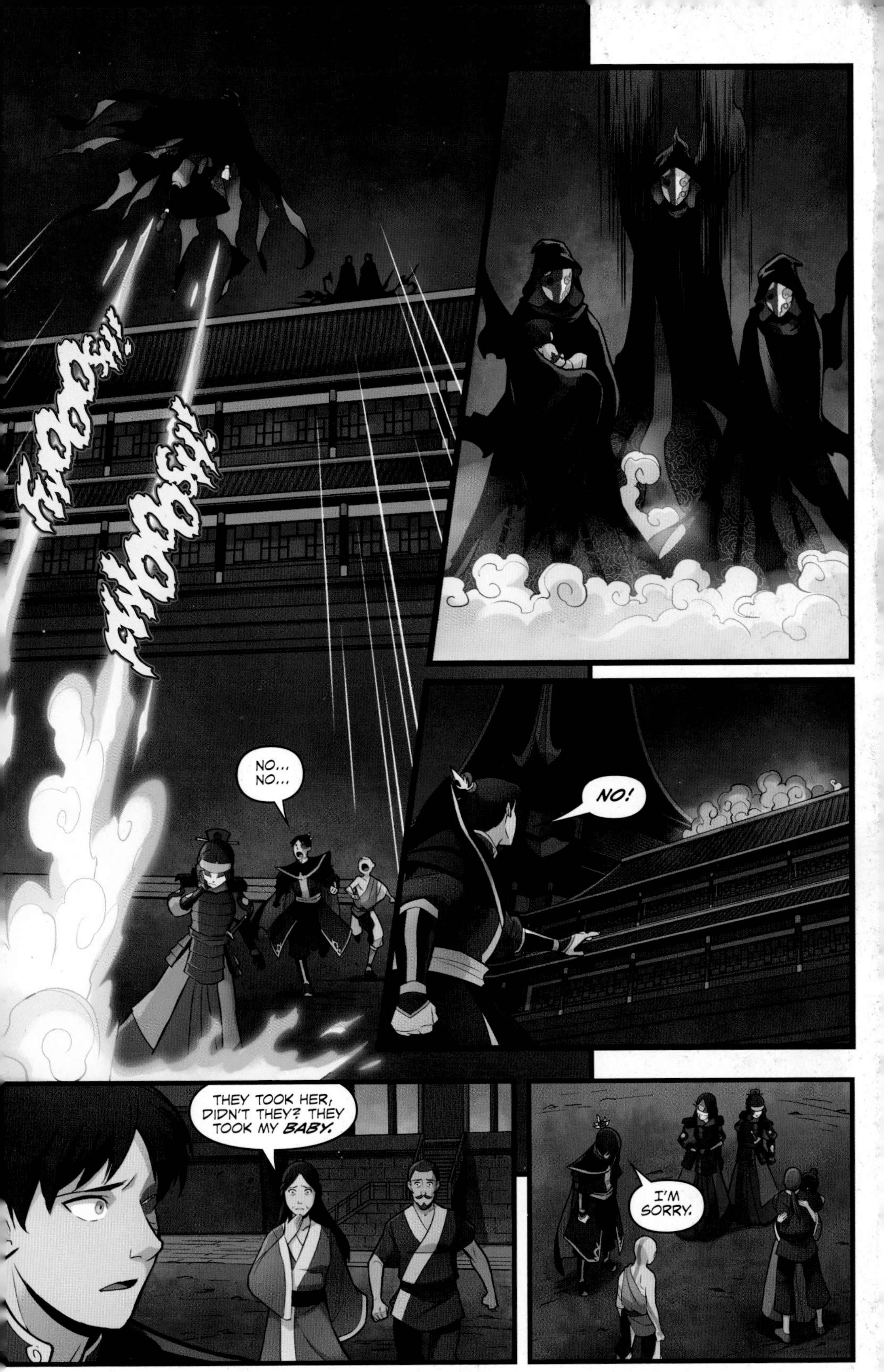
FWOOSH!
FWOOSH!
NO... NO...
NO!
THEY TOOK HER, DIDN'T THEY? THEY TOOK MY *BABY.*
I'M SORRY.

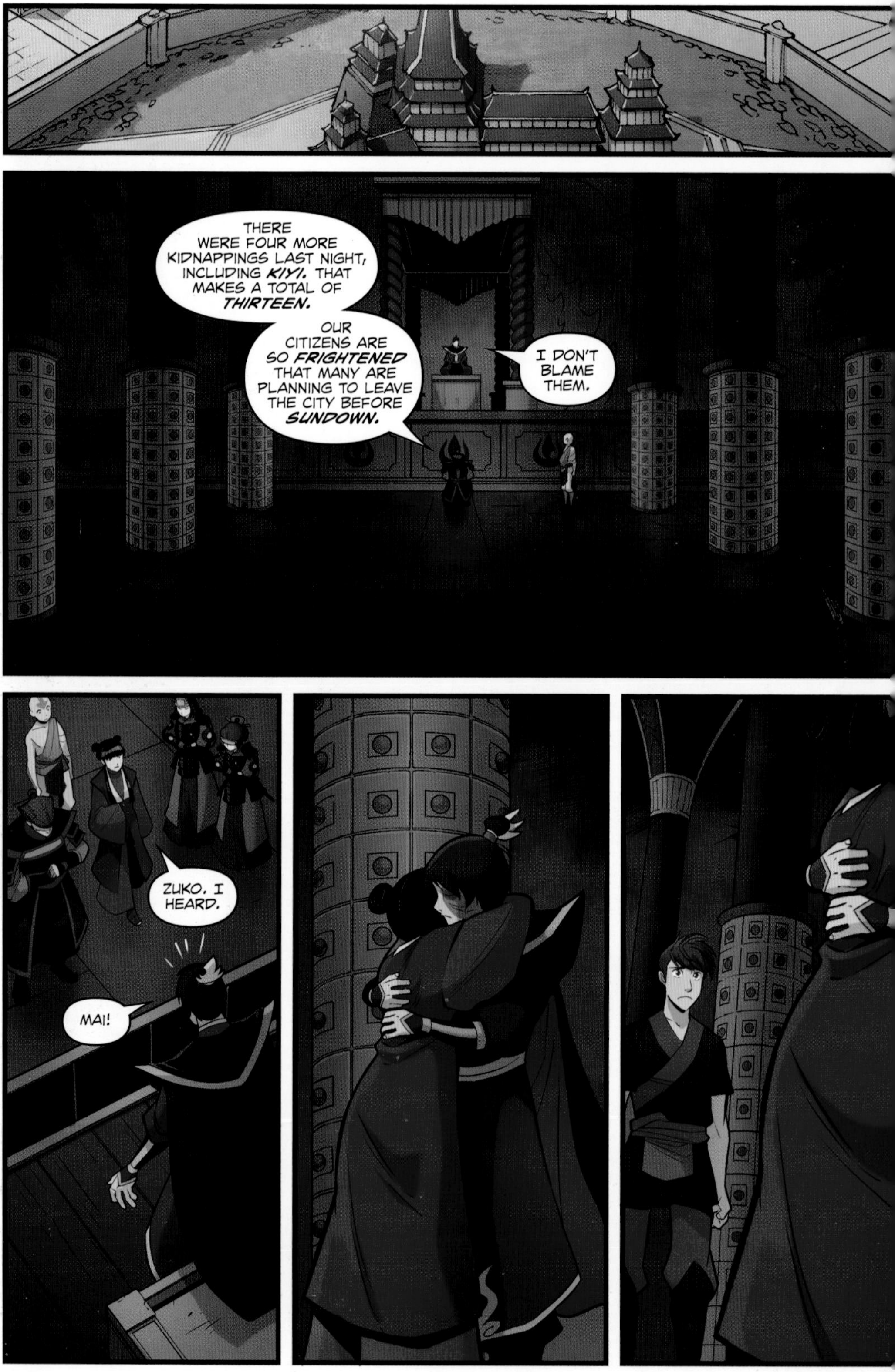
THERE WERE FOUR MORE KIDNAPPINGS LAST NIGHT, INCLUDING KIYI. THAT MAKES A TOTAL OF THIRTEEN.
OUR CITIZENS ARE SO FRIGHTENED THAT MANY ARE PLANNING TO LEAVE THE CITY BEFORE SUNDOWN.
I DON'T BLAME THEM.
ZUKO. I HEARD.
MAI!

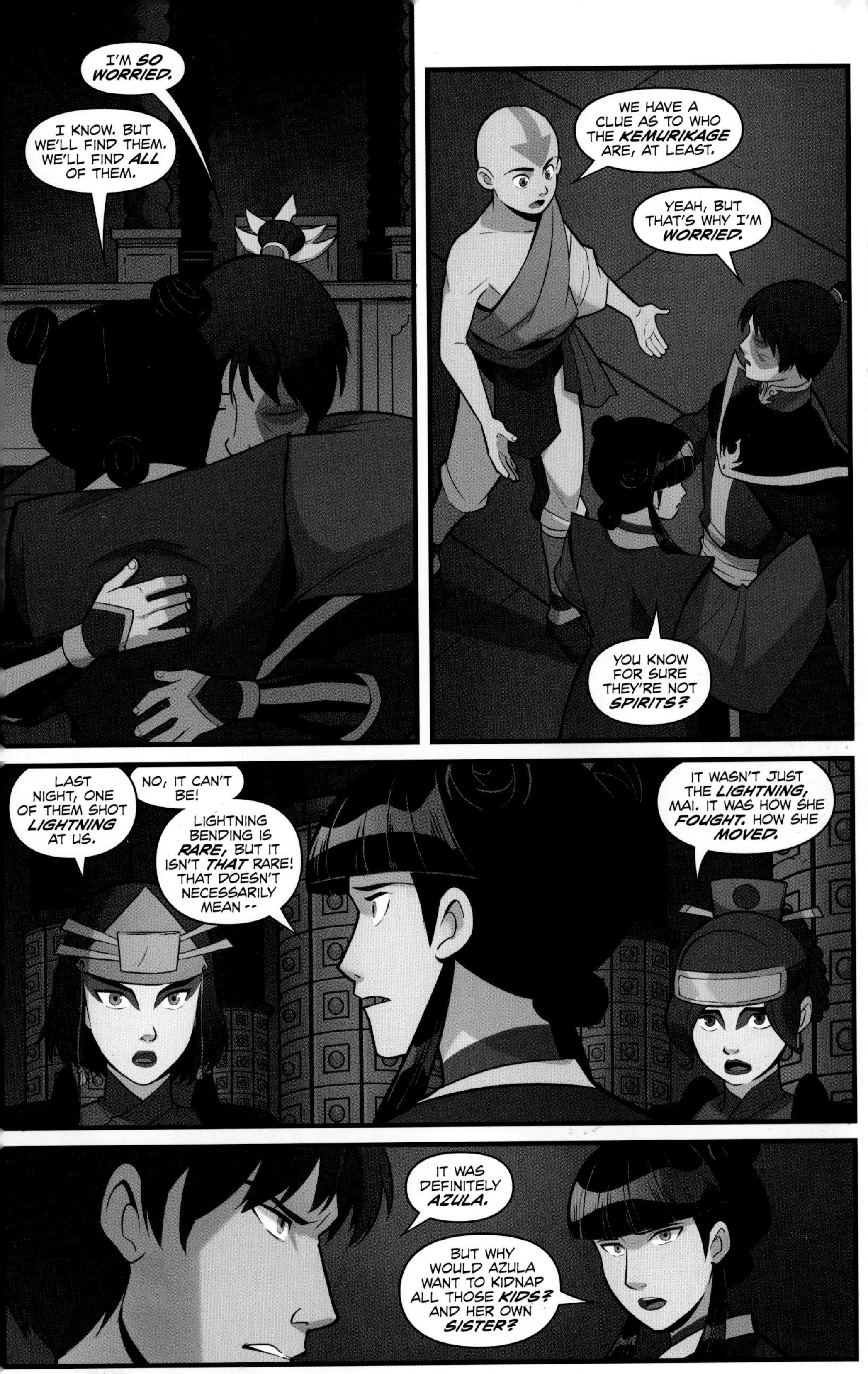
I'M SO WORRIED.
I KNOW. BUT WE'LL FIND THEM. WE'LL FIND ALL OF THEM.
WE HAVE A CLUE AS TO WHO THE KEMURIKAGE ARE, AT LEAST.
YEAH, BUT THAT'S WHY I'M WORRIED.
YOU KNOW FOR SURE THEY'RE NOT SPIRITS?
LAST NIGHT, ONE OF THEM SHOT LIGHTNING AT US.
NO, IT CAN'T BE!
LIGHTNING BENDING IS RARE, BUT IT ISN'T THAT RARE! THAT DOESN'T NECESSARILY MEAN --
IT WASN'T JUST THE LIGHTNING, MAI. IT WAS HOW SHE FOUGHT. HOW SHE MOVED.
IT WAS DEFINITELY AZULA.
BUT WHY WOULD AZULA WANT TO KIDNAP ALL THOSE KIDS? AND HER OWN SISTER?

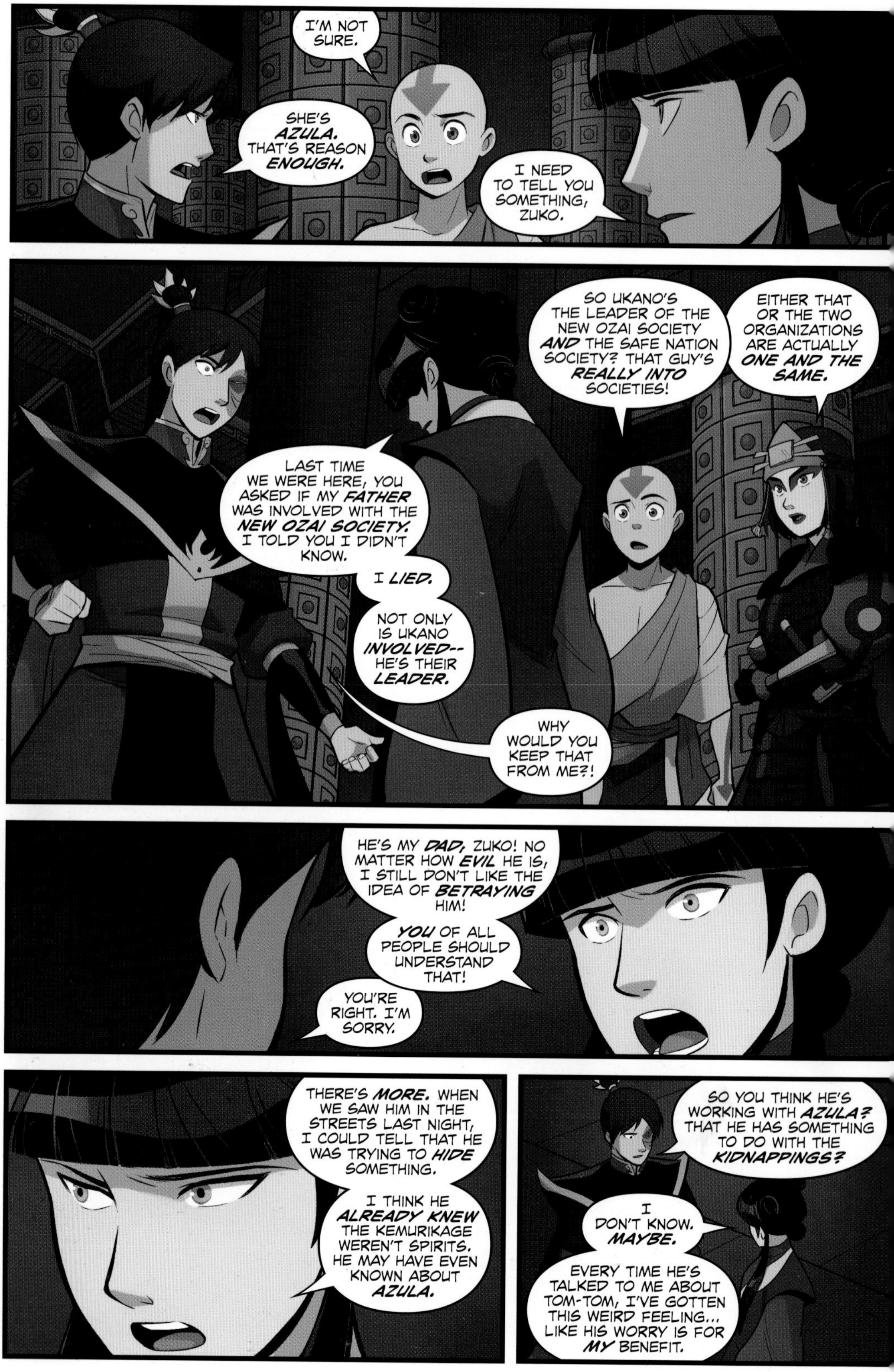
I'M NOT SURE.
SHE'S AZULA. THAT'S REASON ENOUGH.
I NEED TO TELL YOU SOMETHING, ZUKO.
LAST TIME WE WERE HERE, YOU ASKED IF MY FATHER WAS INVOLVED WITH THE NEW OZAI SOCIETY. I TOLD YOU I DIDN'T KNOW.
I LIED.
NOT ONLY IS UKANO INVOLVED-- HE'S THEIR LEADER.
SO UKANO'S THE LEADER OF THE NEW OZAI SOCIETY AND THE SAFE NATION SOCIETY? THAT GUY'S REALLY INTO SOCIETIES!
EITHER THAT OR THE TWO ORGANIZATIONS ARE ACTUALLY ONE AND THE SAME.
WHY WOULD YOU KEEP THAT FROM ME?!
HE'S MY DAD, ZUKO! NO MATTER HOW EVIL HE IS, I STILL DON'T LIKE THE IDEA OF BETRAYING HIM!
YOU OF ALL PEOPLE SHOULD UNDERSTAND THAT!
YOU'RE RIGHT. I'M SORRY.
THERE'S MORE. WHEN WE SAW HIM IN THE STREETS LAST NIGHT, I COULD TELL THAT HE WAS TRYING TO HIDE SOMETHING.
I THINK HE ALREADY KNEW THE KEMURIKAGE WEREN'T SPIRITS. HE MAY HAVE EVEN KNOWN ABOUT AZULA.
SO YOU THINK HE'S WORKING WITH AZULA? THAT HE HAS SOMETHING TO DO WITH THE KIDNAPPINGS?
I DON'T KNOW. MAYBE.
EVERY TIME HE'S TALKED TO ME ABOUT TOM-TOM, I'VE GOTTEN THIS WEIRD FEELING... LIKE HIS WORRY IS FOR MY BENEFIT.

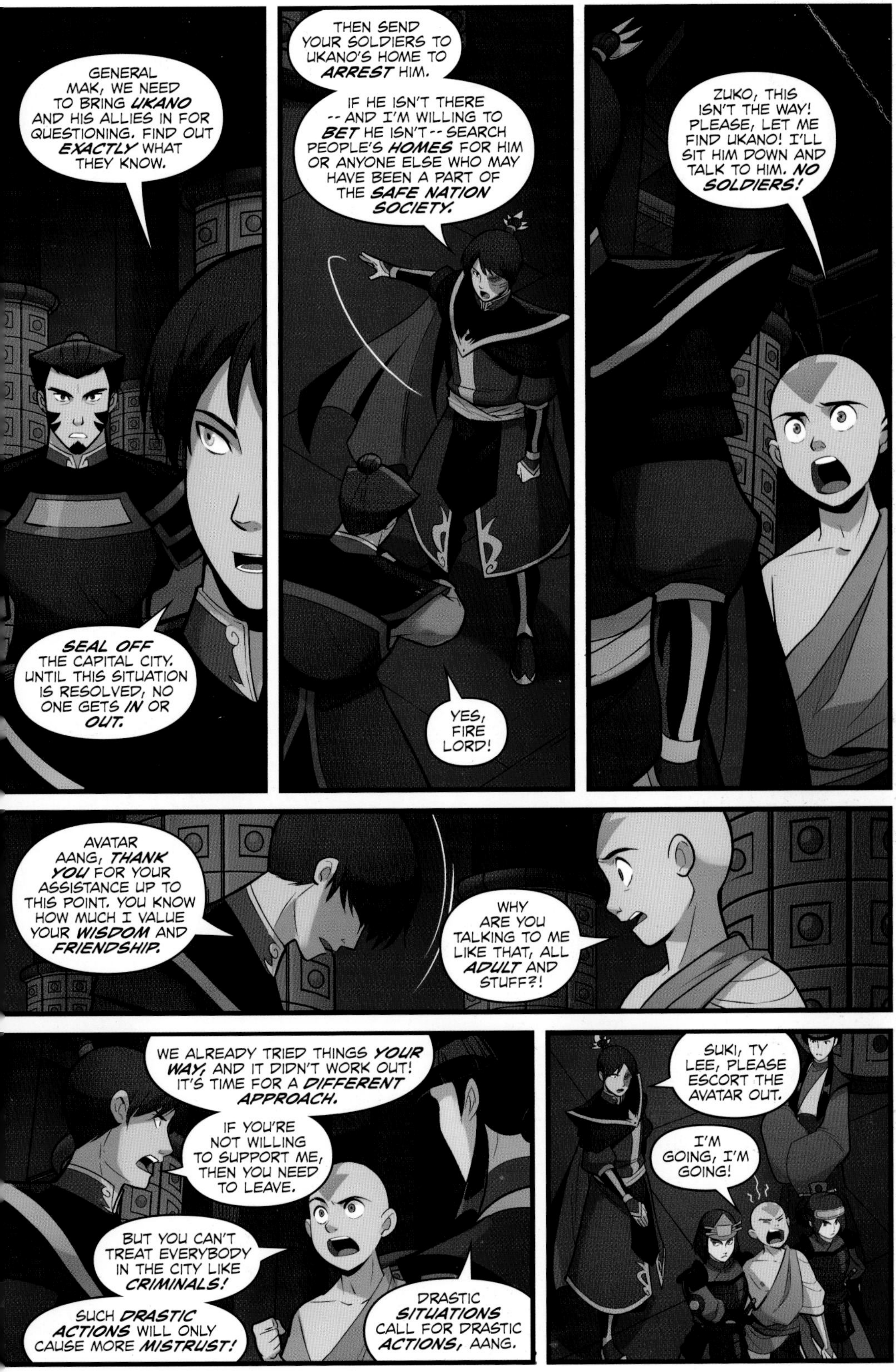
GENERAL MAK, WE NEED TO BRING UKANO AND HIS ALLIES IN FOR QUESTIONING. FIND OUT EXACTLY WHAT THEY KNOW.
SEAL OFF THE CAPITAL CITY. UNTIL THIS SITUATION IS RESOLVED, NO ONE GETS IN OR OUT.
THEN SEND YOUR SOLDIERS TO UKANO'S HOME TO ARREST HIM.
IF HE ISN'T THERE -- AND I'M WILLING TO BET HE ISN'T -- SEARCH PEOPLE'S HOMES FOR HIM OR ANYONE ELSE WHO MAY HAVE BEEN A PART OF THE SAFE NATION SOCIETY.
YES, FIRE LORD!
ZUKO, THIS ISN'T THE WAY! PLEASE, LET ME FIND UKANO! I'LL SIT HIM DOWN AND TALK TO HIM. NO SOLDIERS!
AVATAR AANG, THANK YOU FOR YOUR ASSISTANCE UP TO THIS POINT. YOU KNOW HOW MUCH I VALUE YOUR WISDOM AND FRIENDSHIP.
WHY ARE YOU TALKING TO ME LIKE THAT, ALL ADULT AND STUFF?!
WE ALREADY TRIED THINGS YOUR WAY, AND IT DIDN'T WORK OUT! IT'S TIME FOR A DIFFERENT APPROACH.
IF YOU'RE NOT WILLING TO SUPPORT ME, THEN YOU NEED TO LEAVE.
BUT YOU CAN'T TREAT EVERYBODY IN THE CITY LIKE CRIMINALS!
SUCH DRASTIC ACTIONS WILL ONLY CAUSE MORE MISTRUST!
DRASTIC SITUATIONS CALL FOR DRASTIC ACTIONS, AANG.
SUKI, TY LEE, PLEASE ESCORT THE AVATAR OUT.
I'M GOING, I'M GOING!

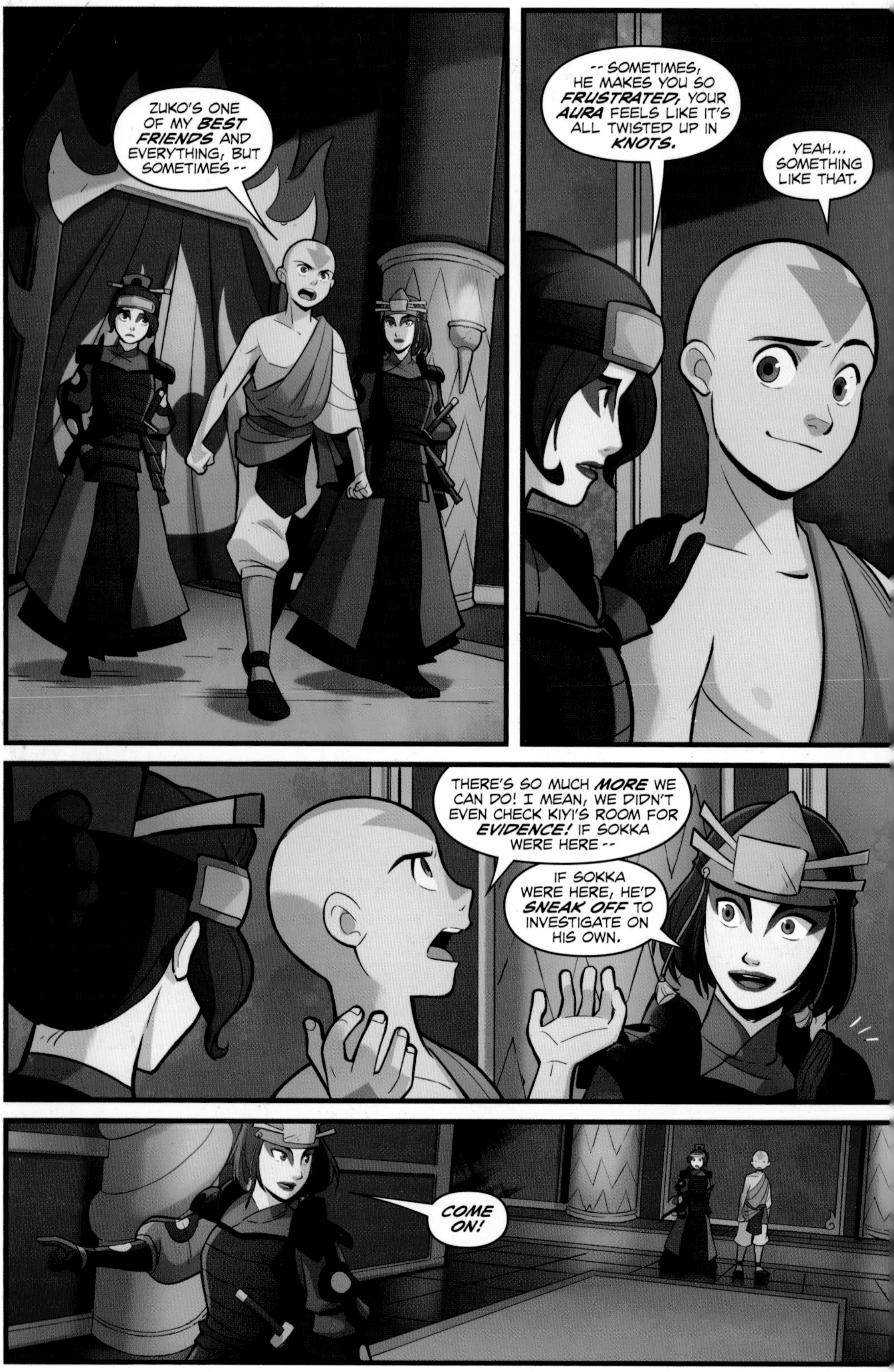
ZUKO'S ONE OF MY BEST FRIENDS AND EVERYTHING, BUT SOMETIMES --
-- SOMETIMES, HE MAKES YOU SO FRUSTRATED, YOUR AURA FEELS LIKE IT'S ALL TWISTED UP IN KNOTS.
YEAH... SOMETHING LIKE THAT.
THERE'S SO MUCH MORE WE CAN DO! I MEAN, WE DIDN'T EVEN CHECK KIYI'S ROOM FOR EVIDENCE! IF SOKKA WERE HERE --
IF SOKKA WERE HERE, HE'D SNEAK OFF TO INVESTIGATE ON HIS OWN.
COME ON!

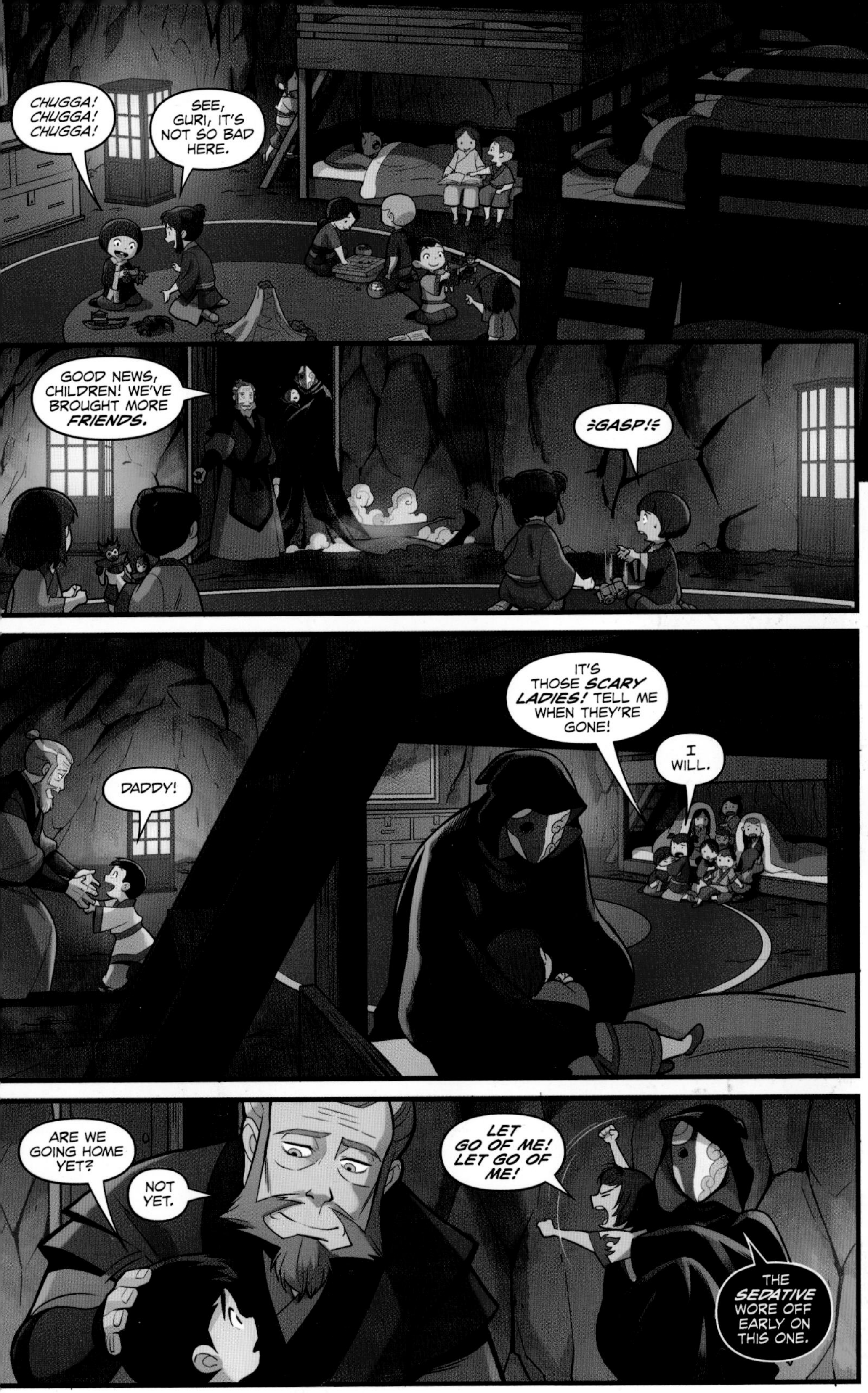
CHUGGA! CHUGGA! CHUGGA!
SEE, GURI, IT'S NOT SO BAD HERE.
GOOD NEWS, CHILDREN! WE'VE BROUGHT MORE FRIENDS.
GASP!
DADDY!
IT'S THOSE SCARY LADIES! TELL ME WHEN THEY'RE GONE!
I WILL.
ARE WE GOING HOME YET?
NOT YET.
LET GO OF ME! LET GO OF ME!
THE SEDATIVE WORE OFF EARLY ON THIS ONE.

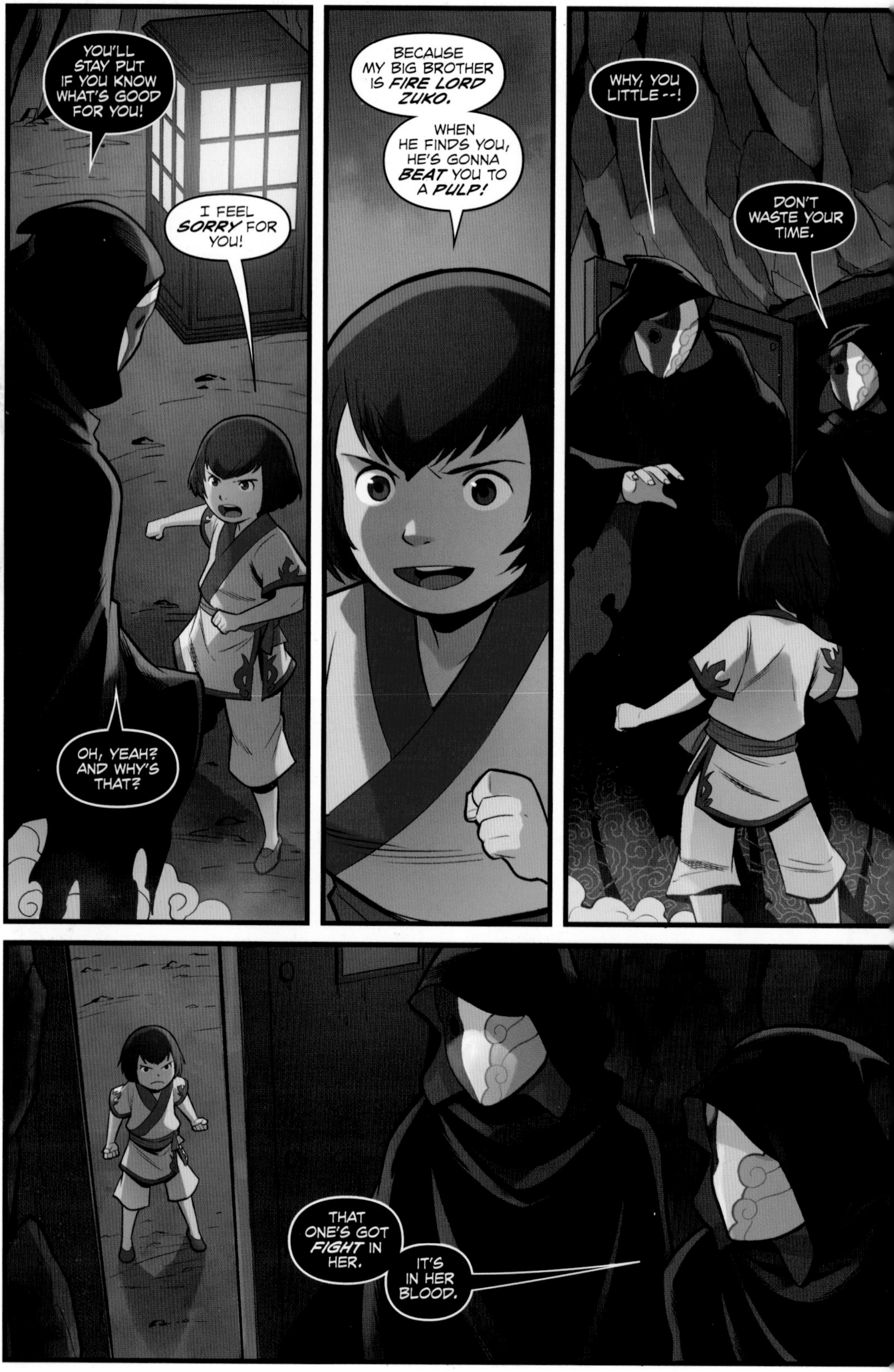
YOU'LL STAY PUT IF YOU KNOW WHAT'S GOOD FOR YOU!
I FEEL SORRY FOR YOU!
OH, YEAH? AND WHY'S THAT?
BECAUSE MY BIG BROTHER IS FIRE LORD ZUKO.
WHEN HE FINDS YOU, HE'S GONNA BEAT YOU TO A PULP!
WHY, YOU LITTLE--!
DON'T WASTE YOUR TIME.
THAT ONE'S GOT FIGHT IN HER.
IT'S IN HER BLOOD.

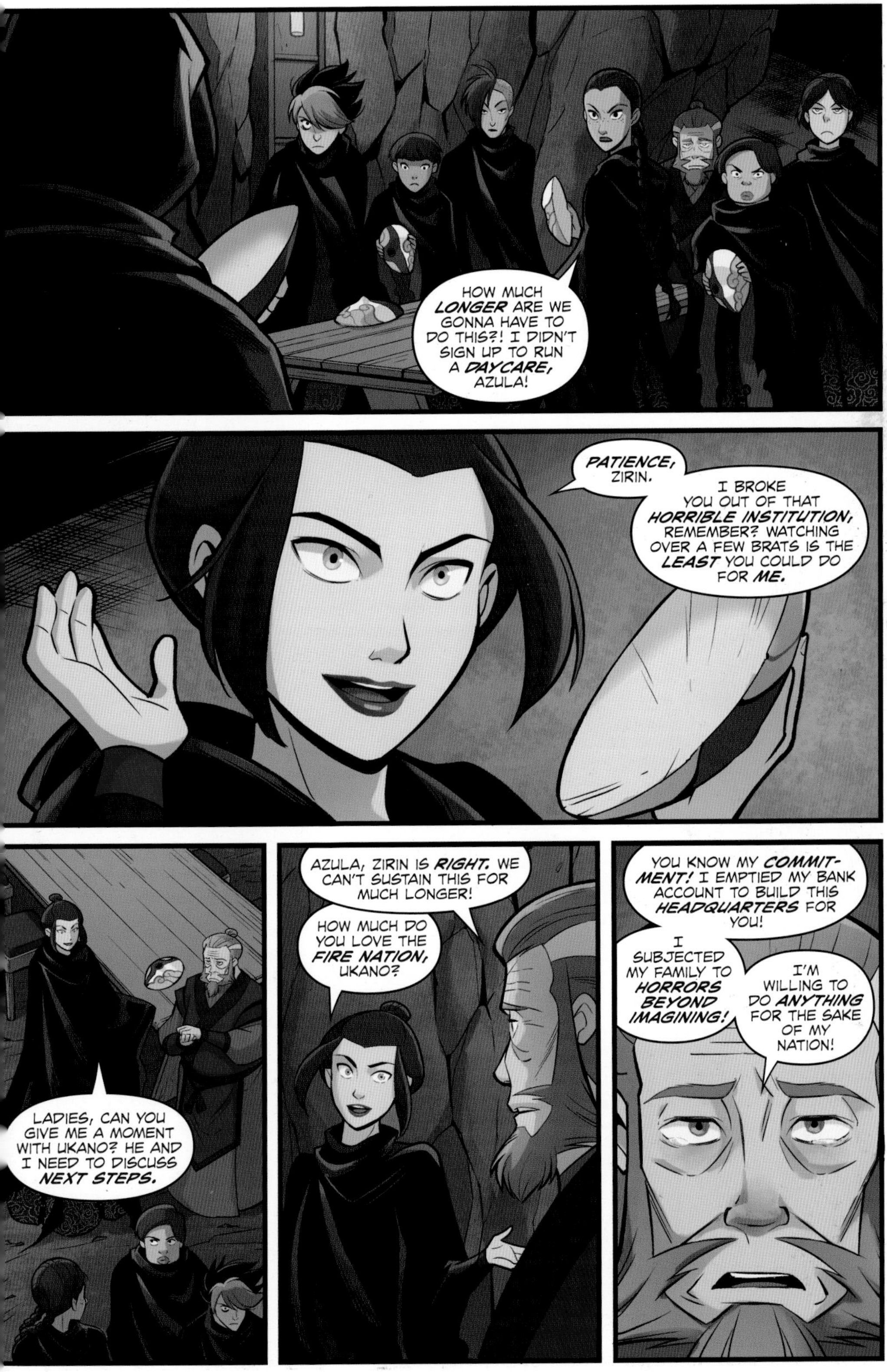

HOW MUCH LONGER ARE WE GONNA HAVE TO DO THIS?! I DIDN'T SIGN UP TO RUN A DAYCARE, AZULA!
PATIENCE, ZIRIN.
I BROKE YOU OUT OF THAT HORRIBLE INSTITUTION, REMEMBER? WATCHING OVER A FEW BRATS IS THE LEAST YOU COULD DO FOR ME.
LADIES, CAN YOU GIVE ME A MOMENT WITH UKANO? HE AND I NEED TO DISCUSS NEXT STEPS.
AZULA, ZIRIN IS RIGHT. WE CAN'T SUSTAIN THIS FOR MUCH LONGER!
HOW MUCH DO YOU LOVE THE FIRE NATION, UKANO?
YOU KNOW MY COMMIT-MENT! I EMPTIED MY BANK ACCOUNT TO BUILD THIS HEADQUARTERS FOR YOU!
I SUBJECTED MY FAMILY TO HORRORS BEYOND IMAGINING!
I'M WILLING TO DO ANYTHING FOR THE SAKE OF MY NATION!

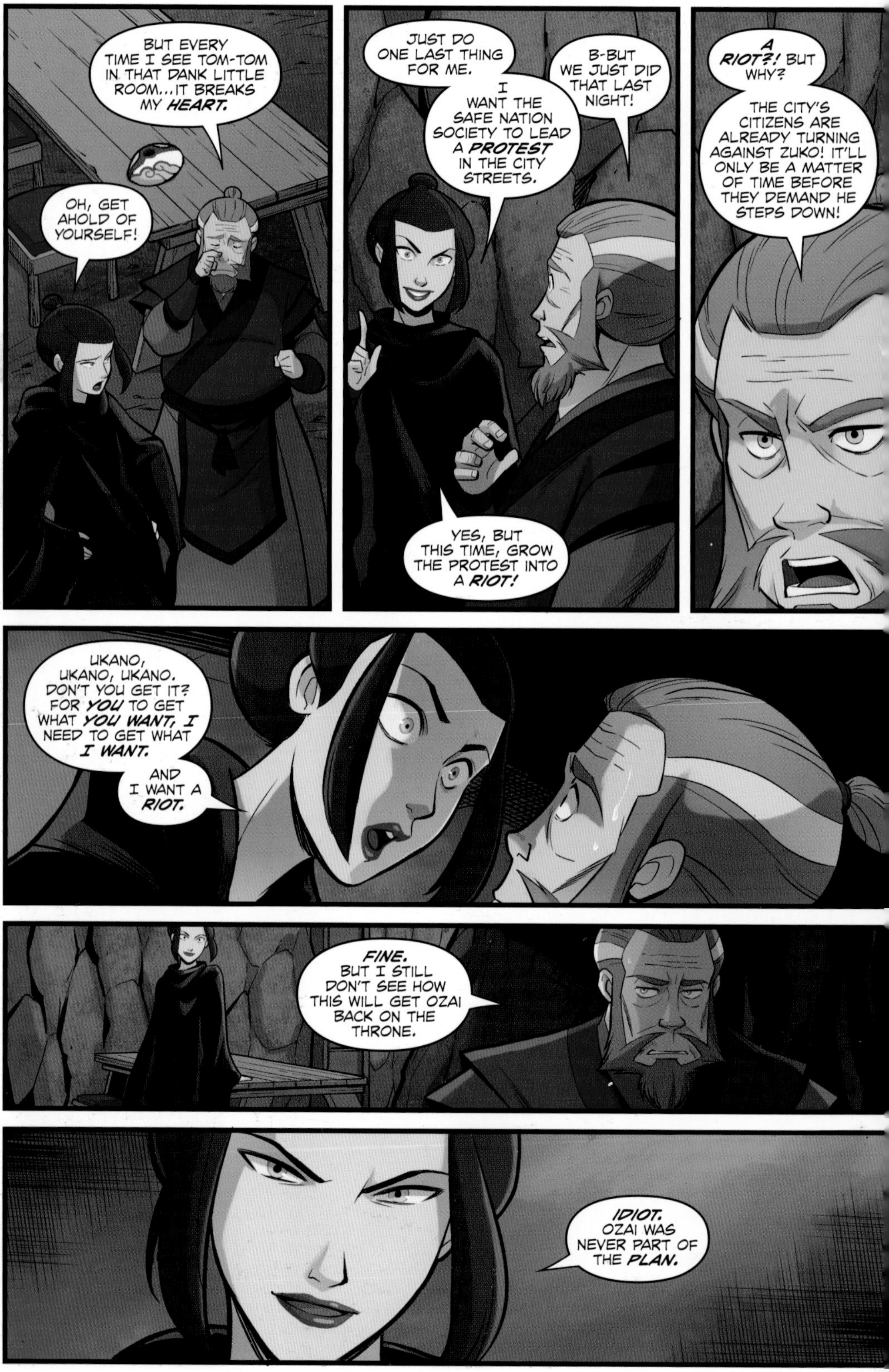
BUT EVERY TIME I SEE TOM-TOM IN THAT DANK LITTLE ROOM...IT BREAKS MY HEART.
OH, GET AHOLD OF YOURSELF!
JUST DO ONE LAST THING FOR ME.
I WANT THE SAFE NATION SOCIETY TO LEAD A PROTEST IN THE CITY STREETS.
B-BUT WE JUST DID THAT LAST NIGHT!
YES, BUT THIS TIME, GROW THE PROTEST INTO A RIOT!
A RIOT?! BUT WHY?
THE CITY'S CITIZENS ARE ALREADY TURNING AGAINST ZUKO! IT'LL ONLY BE A MATTER OF TIME BEFORE THEY DEMAND HE STEPS DOWN!
UKANO, UKANO, UKANO. DON'T YOU GET IT? FOR YOU TO GET WHAT YOU WANT, I NEED TO GET WHAT I WANT.
AND I WANT A RIOT.
FINE. BUT I STILL DON'T SEE HOW THIS WILL GET OZAI BACK ON THE THRONE.
IDIOT. OZAI WAS NEVER PART OF THE PLAN.

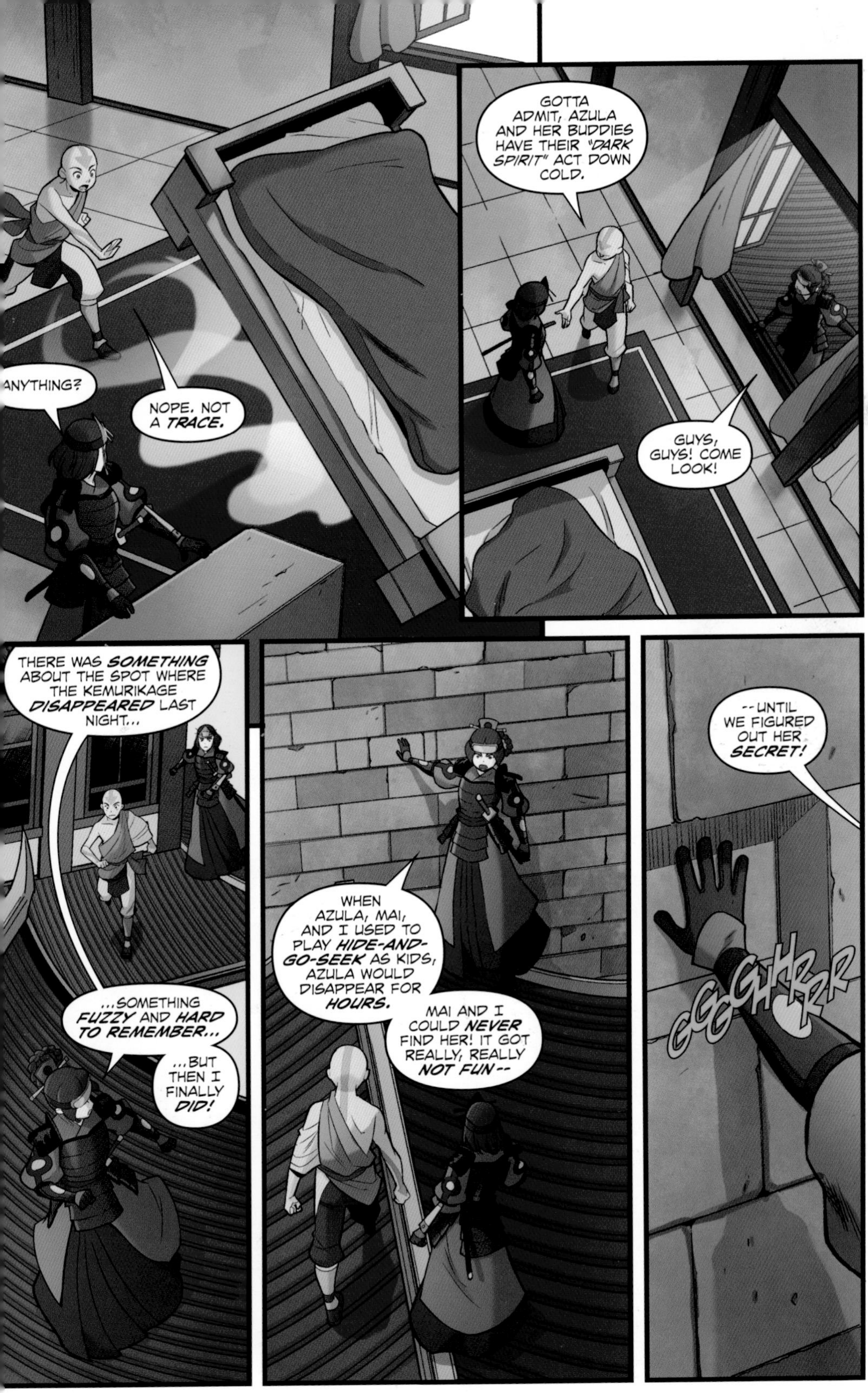
ANYTHING?
NOPE. NOT A TRACE.
GOTTA ADMIT, AZULA AND HER BUDDIES HAVE THEIR "DARK SPIRIT" ACT DOWN COLD.
GUYS, GUYS! COME LOOK!
THERE WAS SOMETHING ABOUT THE SPOT WHERE THE KEMURIKAGE DISAPPEARED LAST NIGHT...
...SOMETHING FUZZY AND HARD TO REMEMBER...
...BUT THEN I FINALLY DID!
WHEN AZULA, MAI, AND I USED TO PLAY HIDE-AND-GO-SEEK AS KIDS, AZULA WOULD DISAPPEAR FOR HOURS.
MAI AND I COULD NEVER FIND HER! IT GOT REALLY, REALLY NOT FUN--
--UNTIL WE FIGURED OUT HER SECRET!
GGGGHRRRR

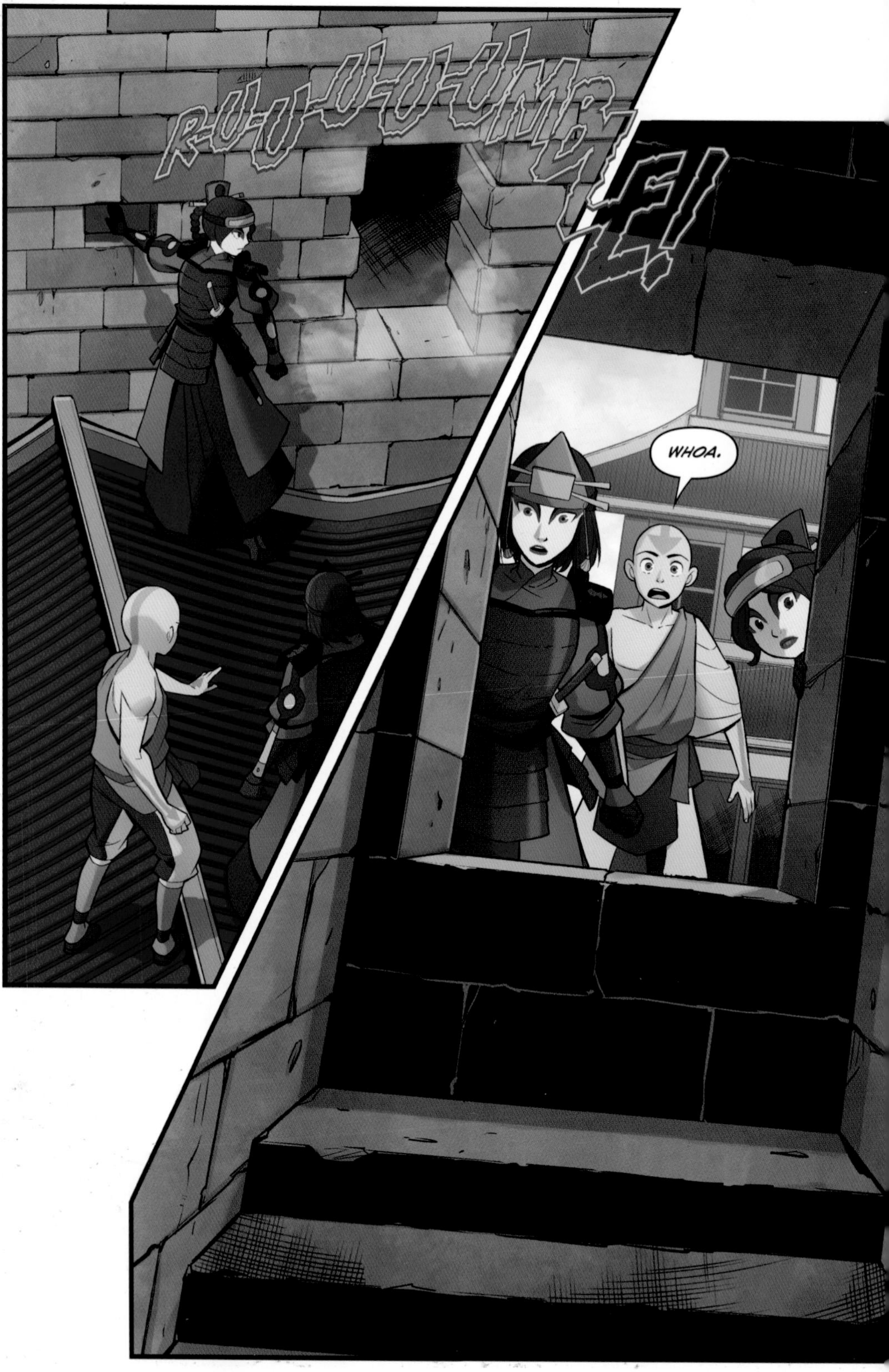
R-U-U-U-U-UMBLE!
WHOA.

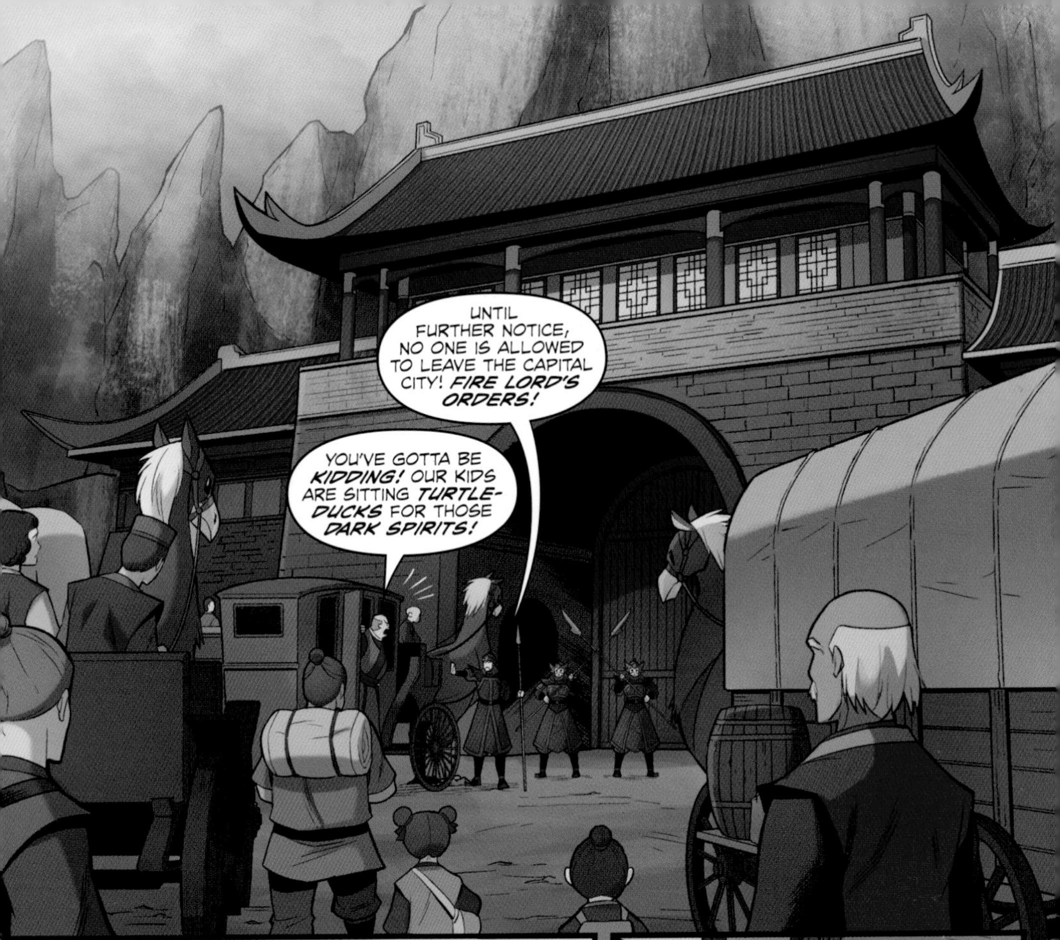
UNTIL FURTHER NOTICE, NO ONE IS ALLOWED TO LEAVE THE CAPITAL CITY! FIRE LORD'S ORDERS!
YOU'VE GOTTA BE KIDDING! OUR KIDS ARE SITTING TURTLE-DUCKS FOR THOSE DARK SPIRITS!

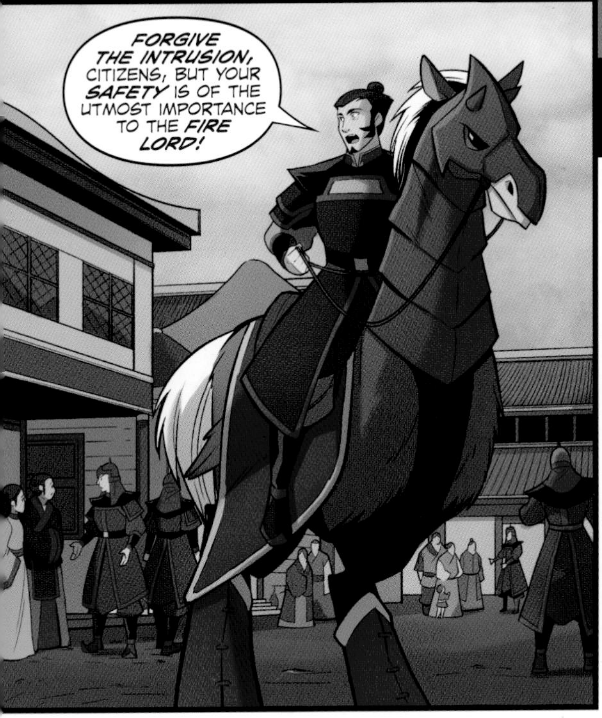
FORGIVE THE INTRUSION, CITIZENS, BUT YOUR SAFETY IS OF THE UTMOST IMPORTANCE TO THE FIRE LORD!

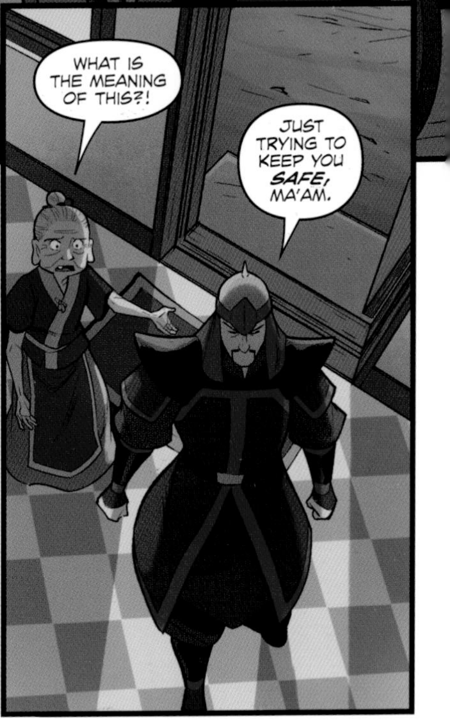
WHAT IS THE MEANING OF THIS?!
JUST TRYING TO KEEP YOU SAFE, MA'AM.

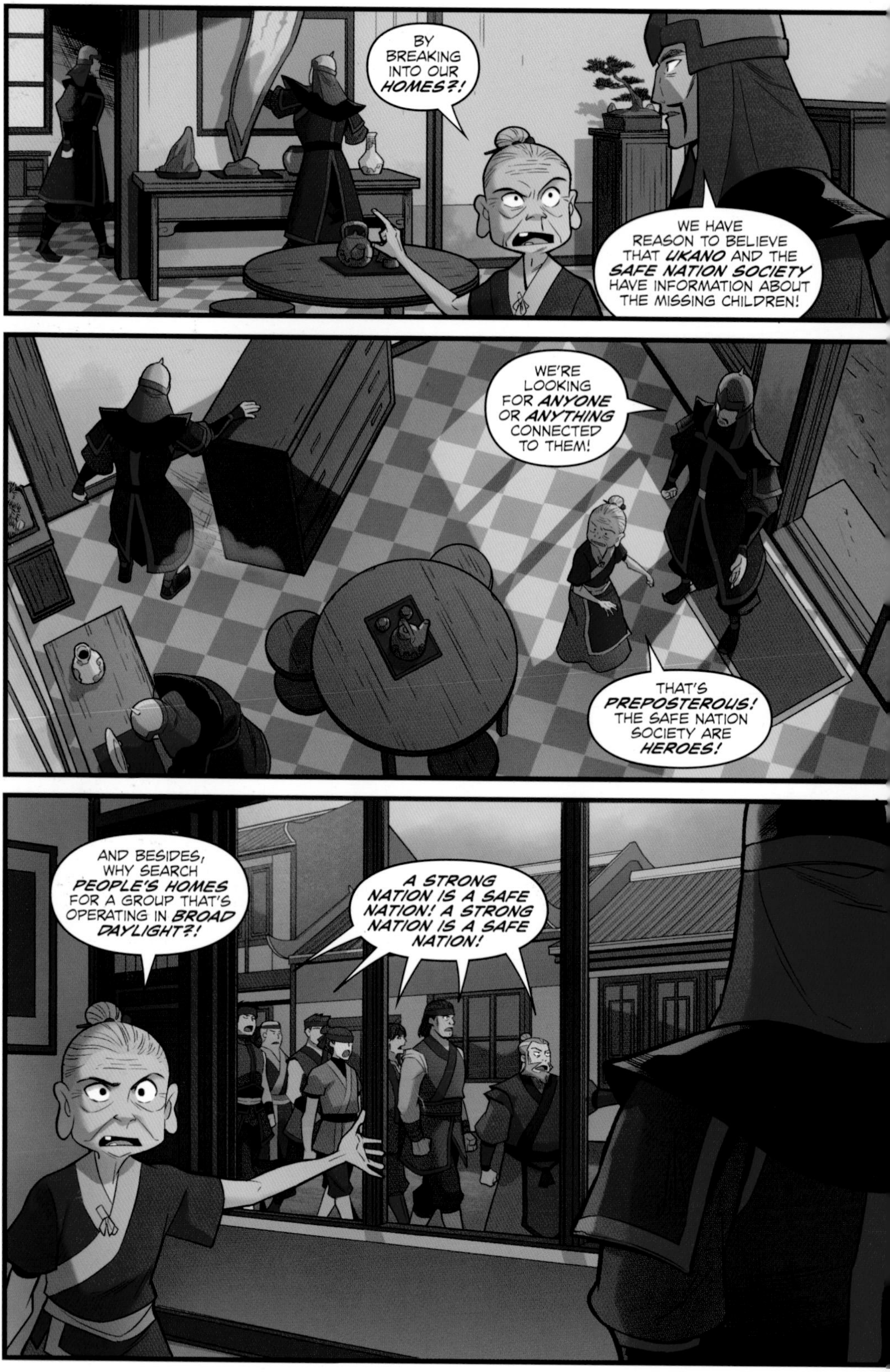
BY BREAKING INTO OUR HOMES?!
WE HAVE REASON TO BELIEVE THAT UKANO AND THE SAFE NATION SOCIETY HAVE INFORMATION ABOUT THE MISSING CHILDREN!
WE'RE LOOKING FOR ANYONE OR ANYTHING CONNECTED TO THEM!
THAT'S PREPOSTEROUS! THE SAFE NATION SOCIETY ARE HEROES!
AND BESIDES, WHY SEARCH PEOPLE'S HOMES FOR A GROUP THAT'S OPERATING IN BROAD DAYLIGHT?!
A STRONG NATION IS A SAFE NATION! A STRONG NATION IS A SAFE NATION!

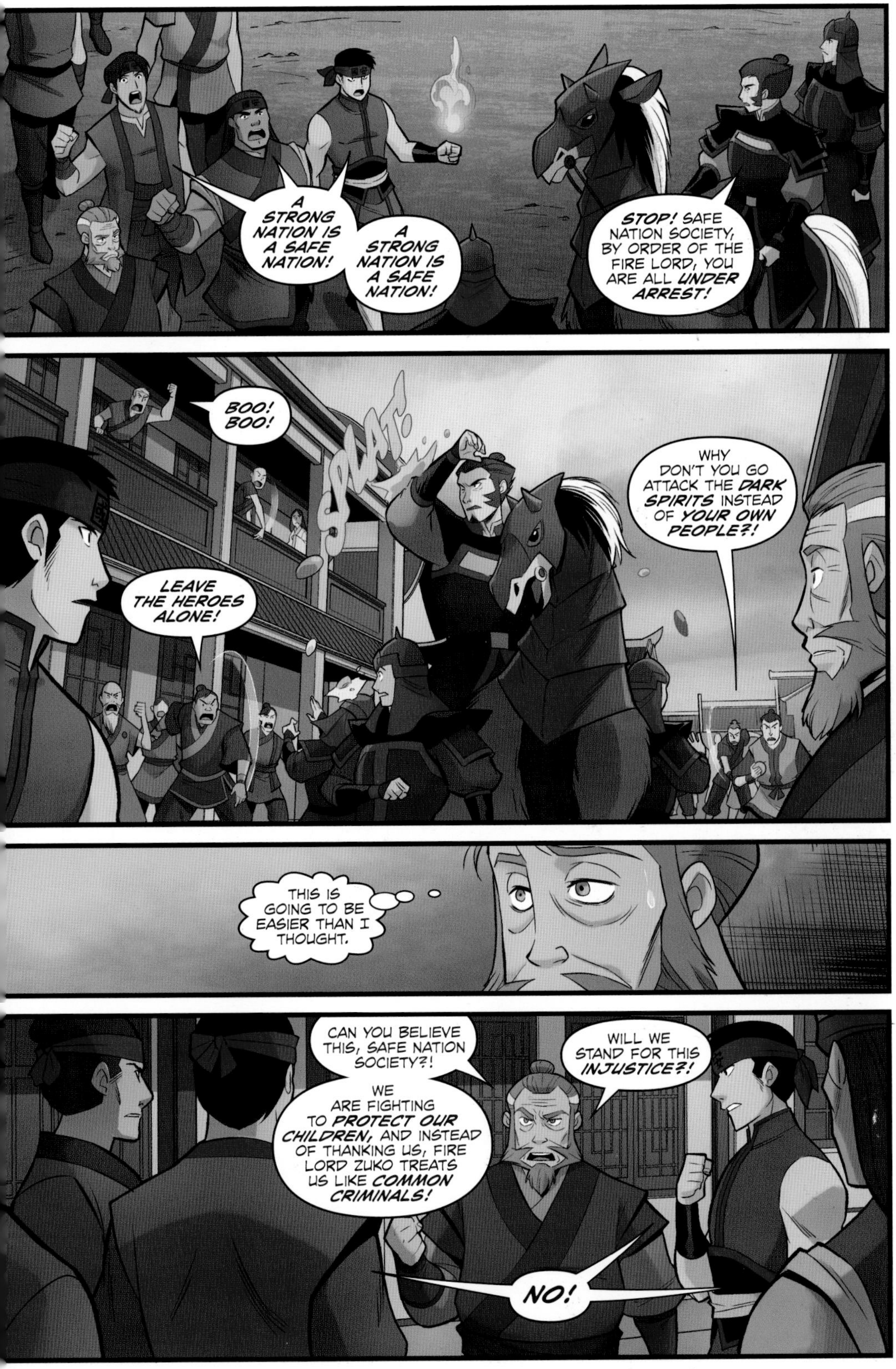
A STRONG NATION IS A SAFE NATION!
A STRONG NATION IS A SAFE NATION!
STOP! SAFE NATION SOCIETY, BY ORDER OF THE FIRE LORD, YOU ARE ALL UNDER ARREST!
BOO! BOO!
SPLAT!
LEAVE THE HEROES ALONE!
WHY DON'T YOU GO ATTACK THE DARK SPIRITS INSTEAD OF YOUR OWN PEOPLE?!
THIS IS GOING TO BE EASIER THAN I THOUGHT.
CAN YOU BELIEVE THIS, SAFE NATION SOCIETY?!
WE ARE FIGHTING TO PROTECT OUR CHILDREN, AND INSTEAD OF THANKING US, FIRE LORD ZUKO TREATS US LIKE COMMON CRIMINALS!
WILL WE STAND FOR THIS INJUSTICE?!
NO!

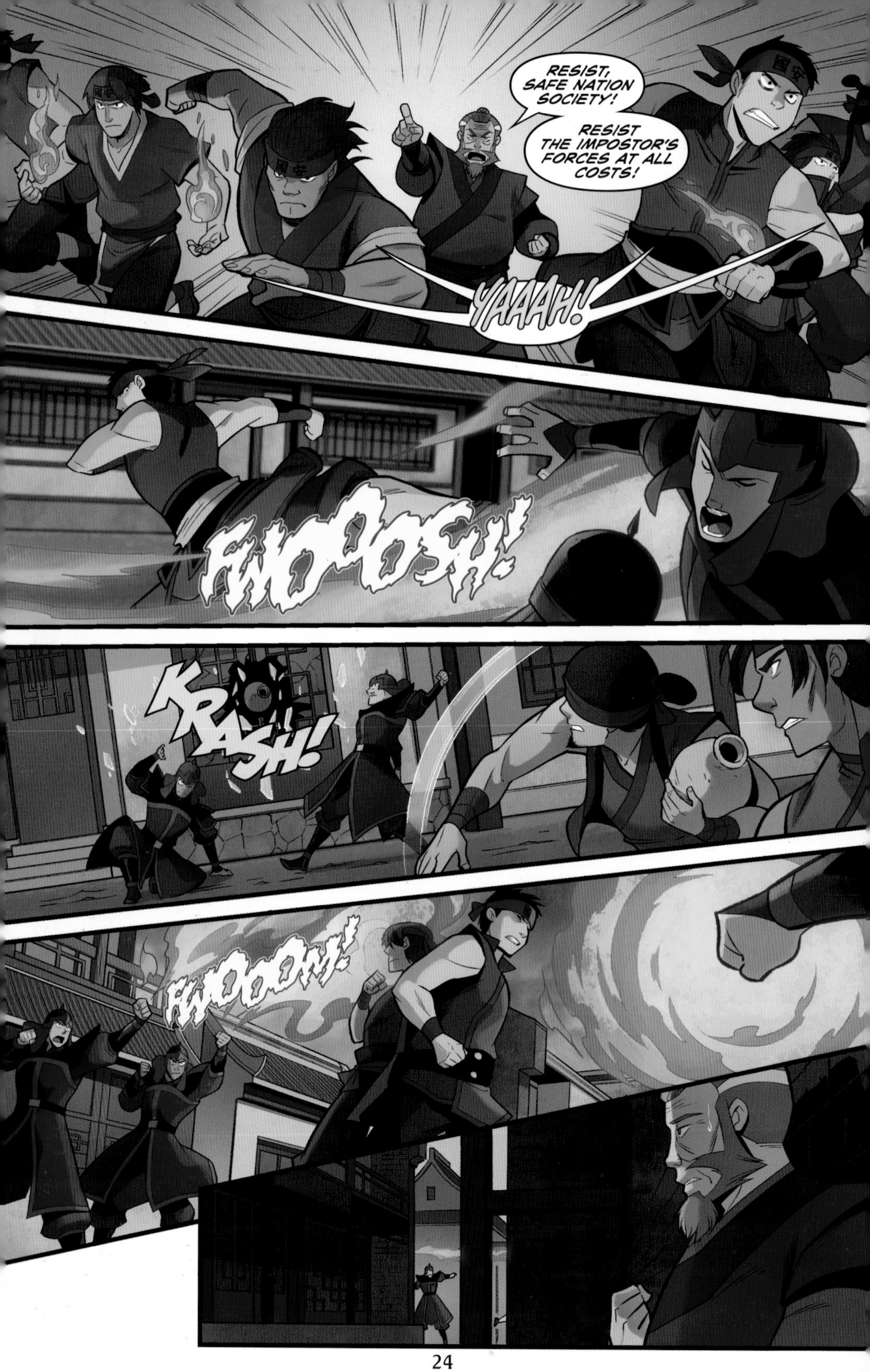
RESIST, SAFE NATION SOCIETY!
RESIST THE IMPOSTOR'S FORCES AT ALL COSTS!
YAAAH!
FWOOOSH!
KRASH!
FWOOOM!

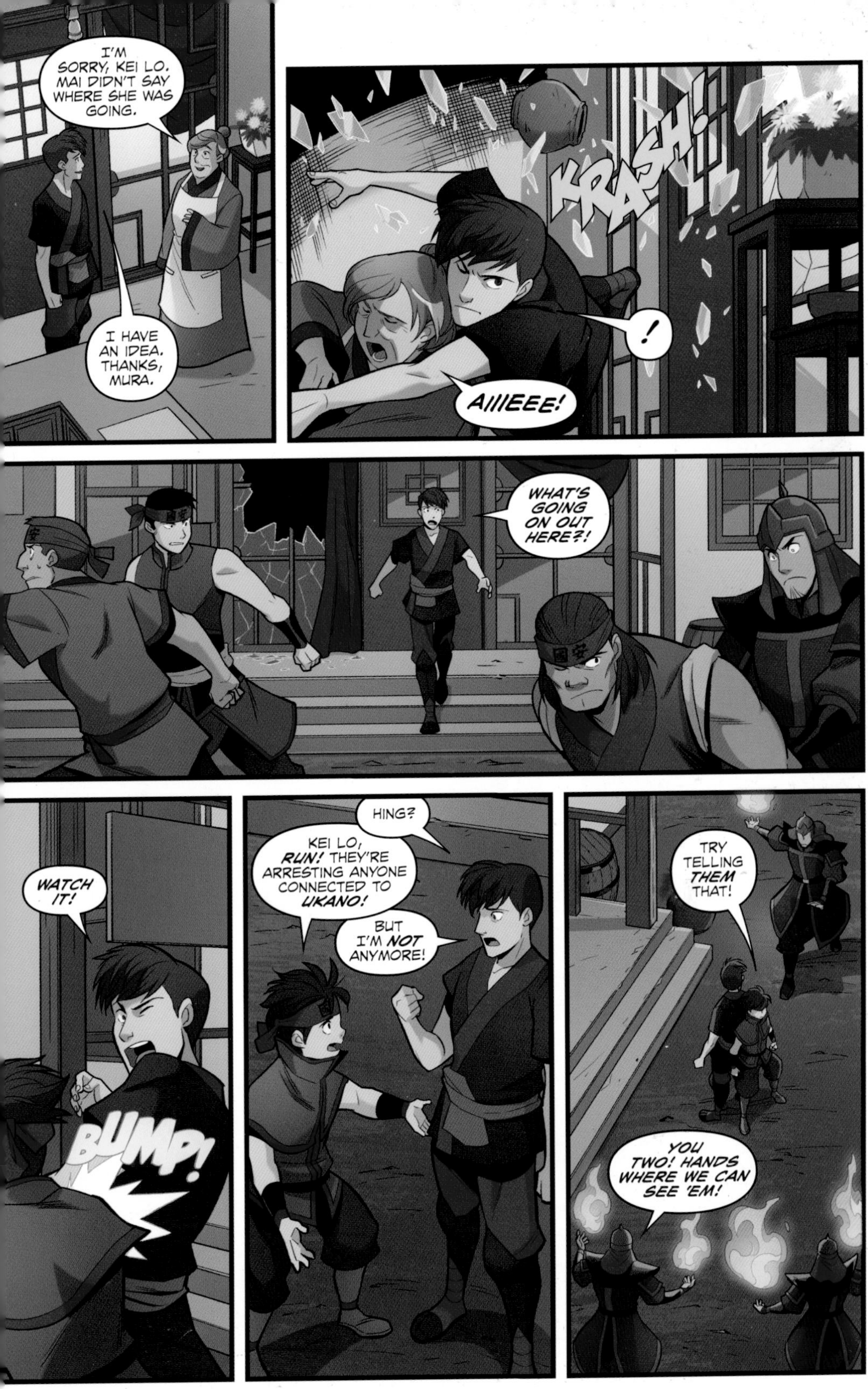
I'M SORRY, KEI LO. MAI DIDN'T SAY WHERE SHE WAS GOING.
I HAVE AN IDEA. THANKS, MURA.
KRASH!!
!
AIIIEEE!
WHAT'S GOING ON OUT HERE?!
WATCH IT!
BUMP!
HING?
KEI LO, RUN! THEY'RE ARRESTING ANYONE CONNECTED TO UKANO!
BUT I'M NOT ANYMORE!
TRY TELLING THEM THAT!
YOU TWO! HANDS WHERE WE CAN SEE 'EM!

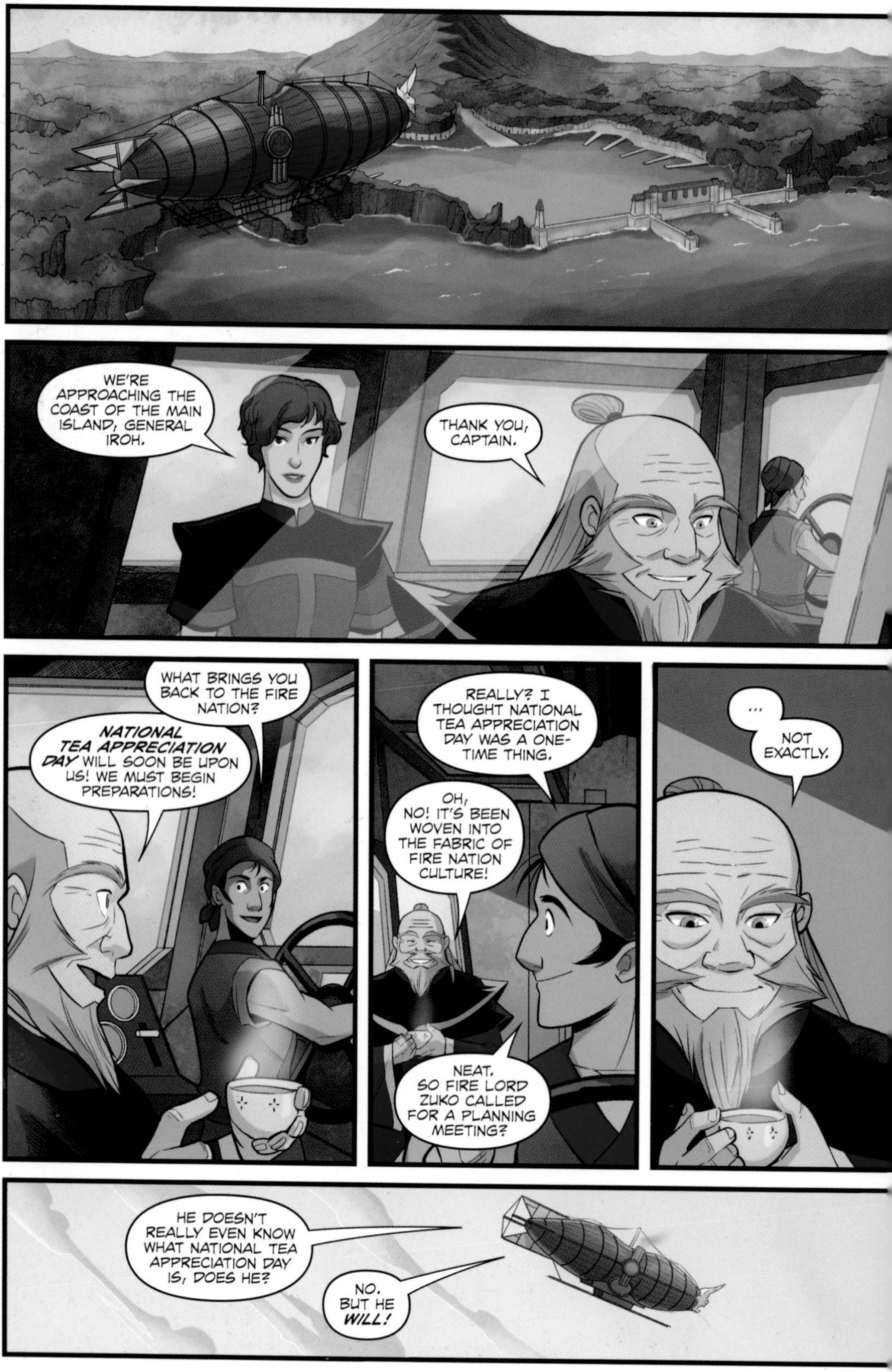
WE'RE APPROACHING THE COAST OF THE MAIN ISLAND, GENERAL IROH.
THANK YOU, CAPTAIN.
WHAT BRINGS YOU BACK TO THE FIRE NATION?
NATIONAL TEA APPRECIATION DAY WILL SOON BE UPON US! WE MUST BEGIN PREPARATIONS!
REALLY? I THOUGHT NATIONAL TEA APPRECIATION DAY WAS A ONE-TIME THING.
OH, NO! IT'S BEEN WOVEN INTO THE FABRIC OF FIRE NATION CULTURE!
NEAT. SO FIRE LORD ZUKO CALLED FOR A PLANNING MEETING?
...
NOT EXACTLY.
HE DOESN'T REALLY EVEN KNOW WHAT NATIONAL TEA APPRECIATION DAY IS, DOES HE?
NO. BUT HE *WILL!*

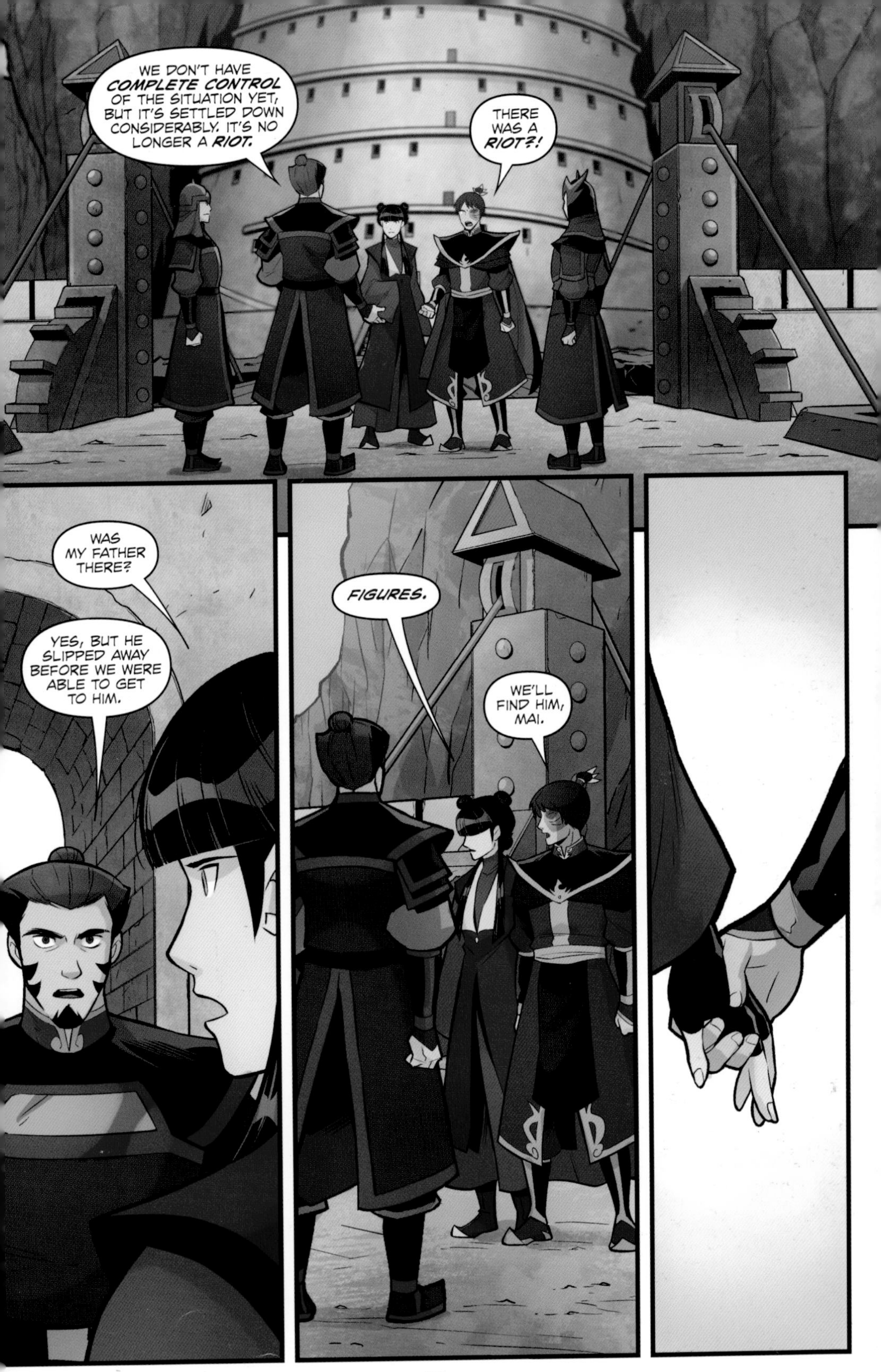
WE DON'T HAVE COMPLETE CONTROL OF THE SITUATION YET, BUT IT'S SETTLED DOWN CONSIDERABLY. IT'S NO LONGER A RIOT.
THERE WAS A RIOT?!
WAS MY FATHER THERE?
YES, BUT HE SLIPPED AWAY BEFORE WE WERE ABLE TO GET TO HIM.
FIGURES.
WE'LL FIND HIM, MAI.

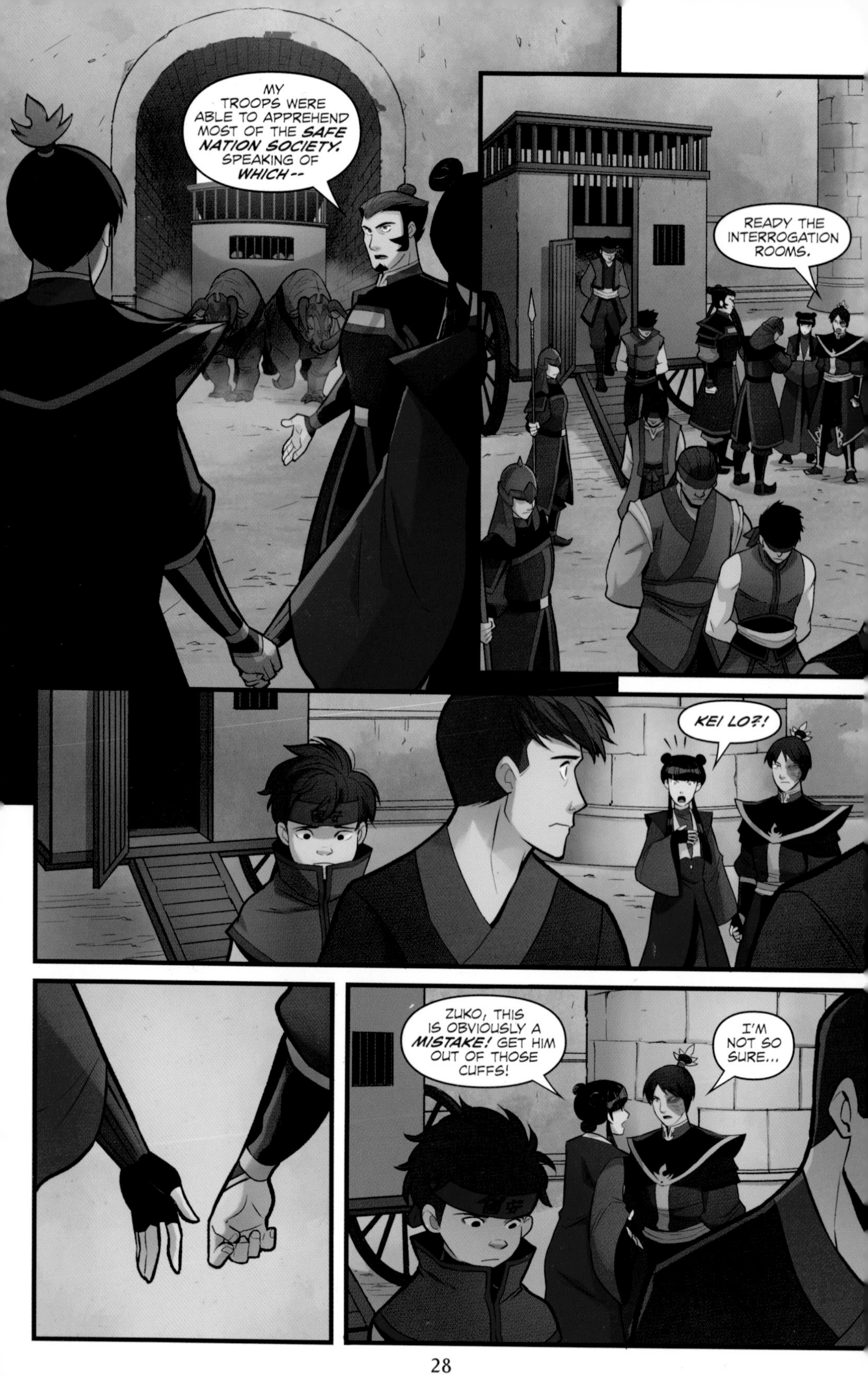
MY TROOPS WERE ABLE TO APPREHEND MOST OF THE SAFE NATION SOCIETY. SPEAKING OF WHICH--
READY THE INTERROGATION ROOMS.
KEI LO?!
ZUKO, THIS IS OBVIOUSLY A MISTAKE! GET HIM OUT OF THOSE CUFFS!
I'M NOT SO SURE...

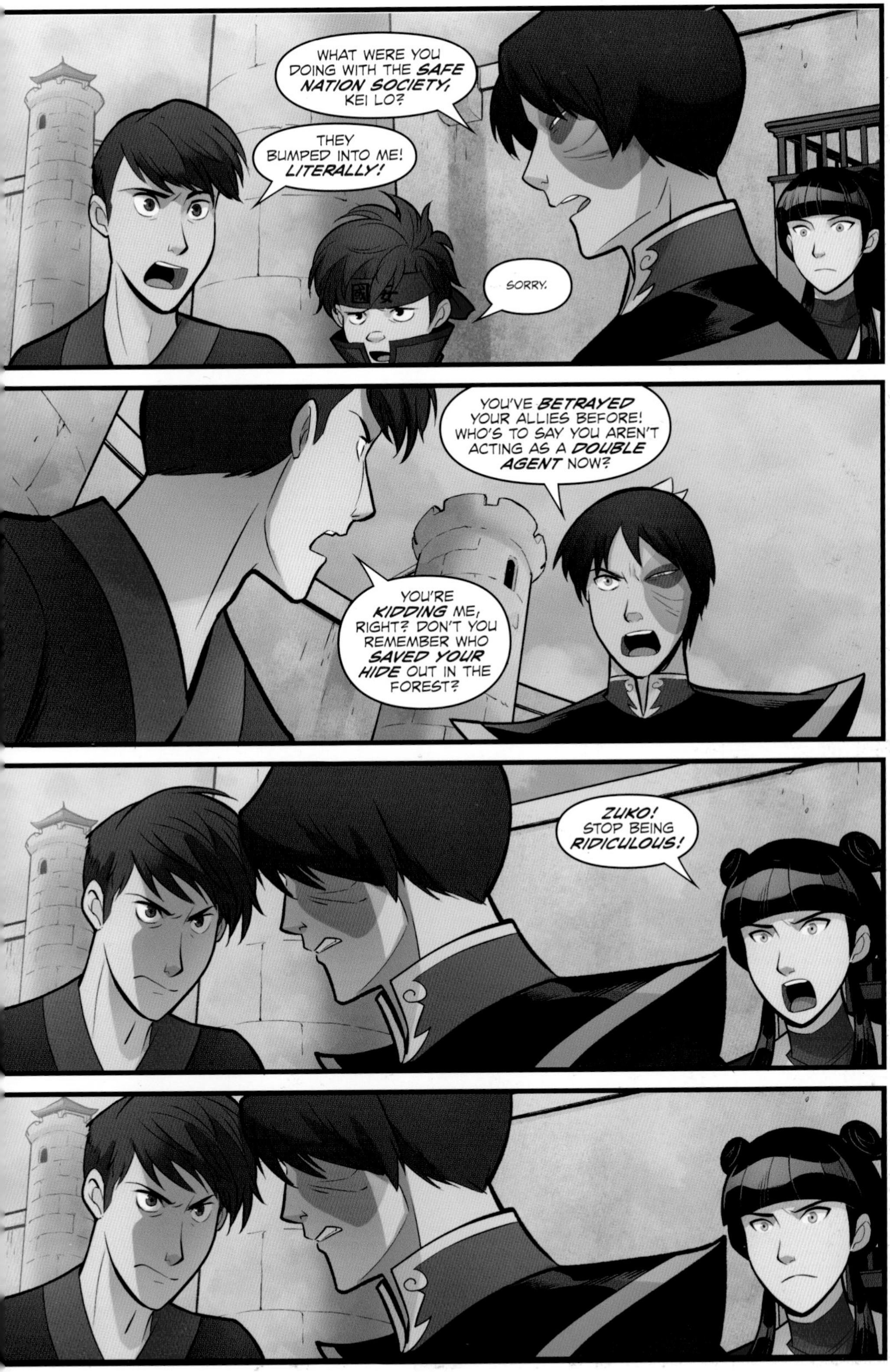
WHAT WERE YOU DOING WITH THE SAFE NATION SOCIETY, KEI LO?
THEY BUMPED INTO ME! LITERALLY!
SORRY.
YOU'VE BETRAYED YOUR ALLIES BEFORE! WHO'S TO SAY YOU AREN'T ACTING AS A DOUBLE AGENT NOW?
YOU'RE KIDDING ME, RIGHT? DON'T YOU REMEMBER WHO SAVED YOUR HIDE OUT IN THE FOREST?
ZUKO! STOP BEING RIDICULOUS!

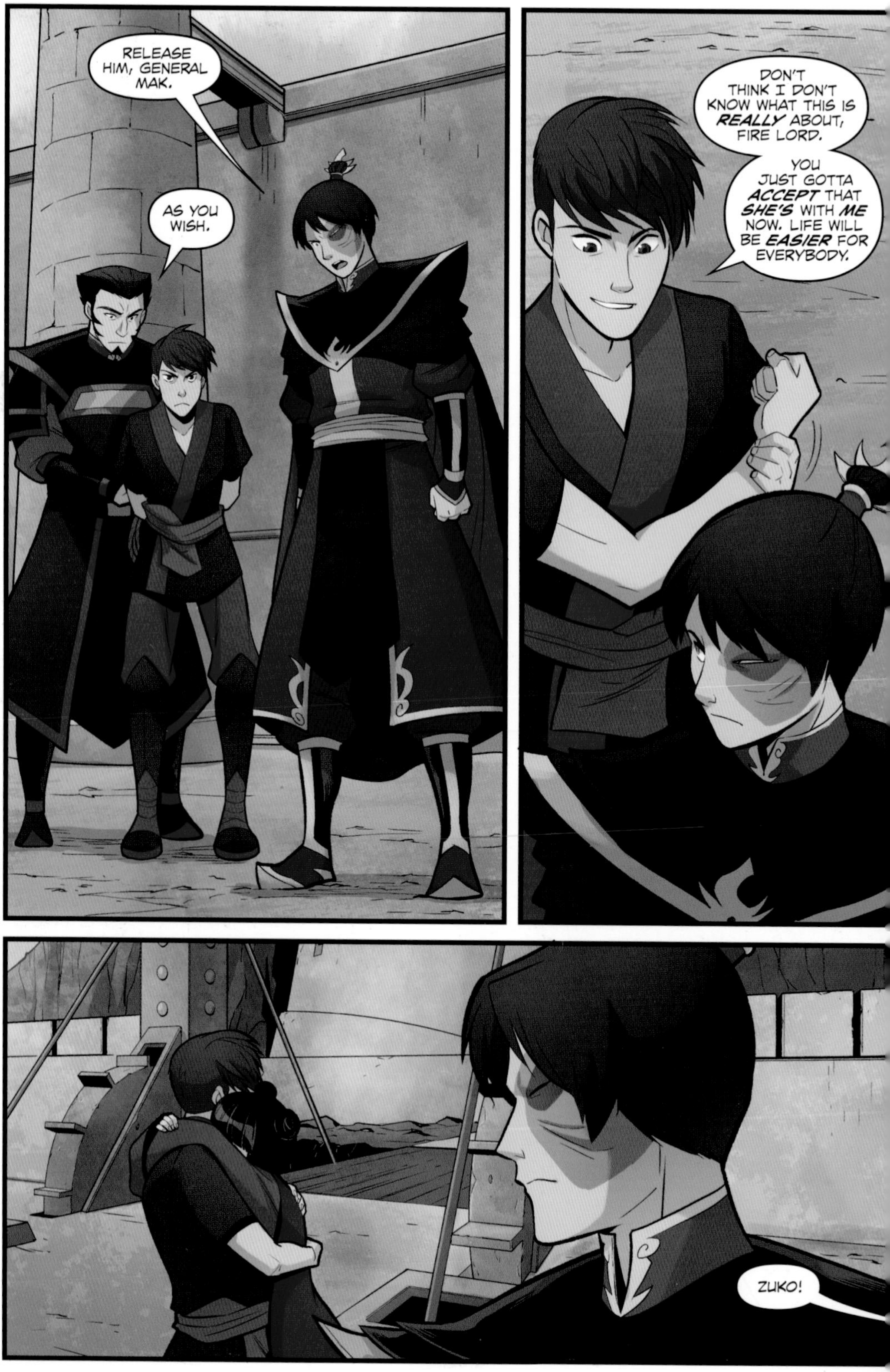
RELEASE HIM, GENERAL MAK.
AS YOU WISH.
DON'T THINK I DON'T KNOW WHAT THIS IS REALLY ABOUT, FIRE LORD.
YOU JUST GOTTA ACCEPT THAT SHE'S WITH ME NOW. LIFE WILL BE EASIER FOR EVERYBODY.
ZUKO!

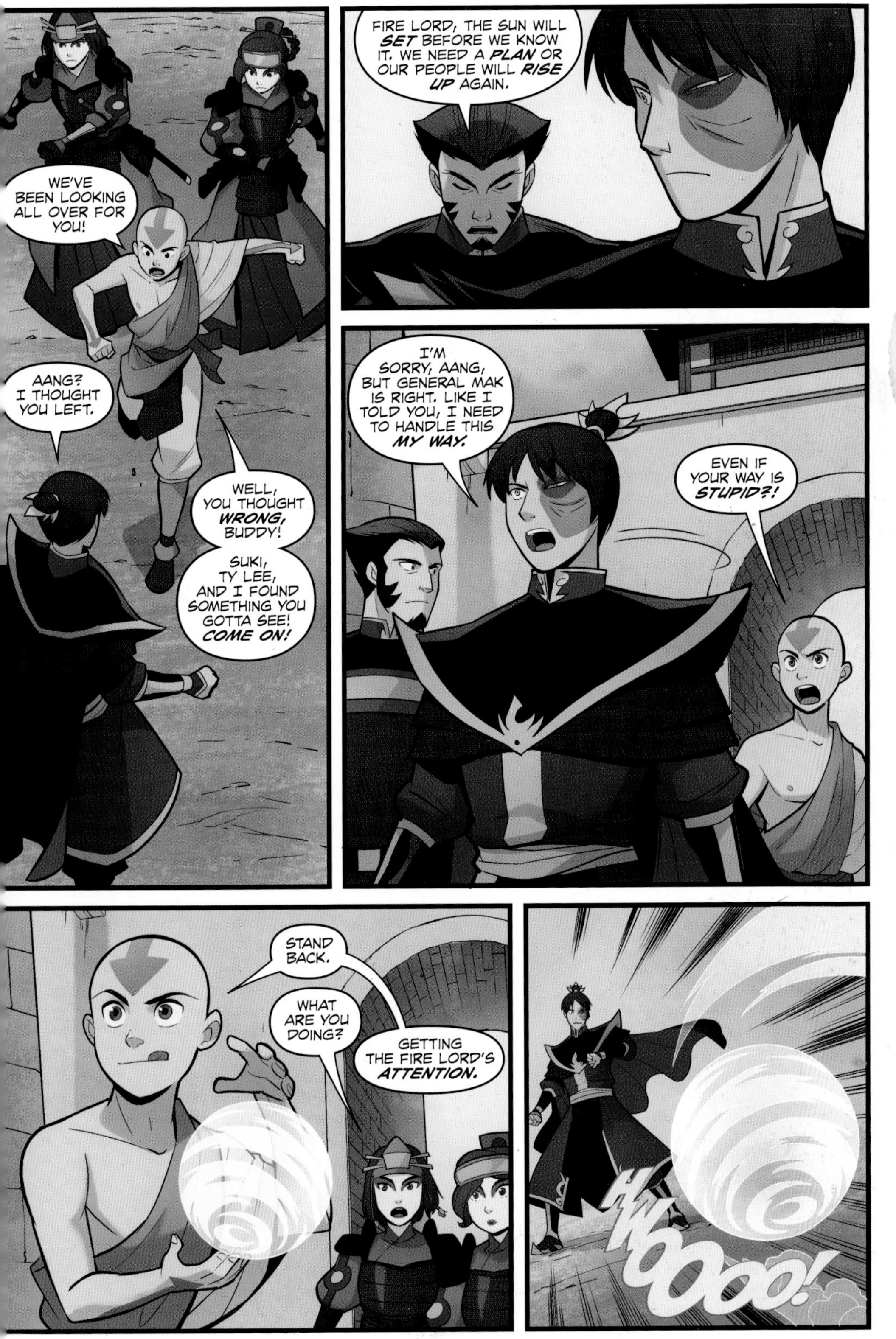

WE'VE BEEN LOOKING ALL OVER FOR YOU!
AANG? I THOUGHT YOU LEFT.
WELL, YOU THOUGHT WRONG, BUDDY!
SUKI, TY LEE, AND I FOUND SOMETHING YOU GOTTA SEE! COME ON!
FIRE LORD, THE SUN WILL SET BEFORE WE KNOW IT. WE NEED A PLAN OR OUR PEOPLE WILL RISE UP AGAIN.
I'M SORRY, AANG, BUT GENERAL MAK IS RIGHT. LIKE I TOLD YOU, I NEED TO HANDLE THIS MY WAY.
EVEN IF YOUR WAY IS STUPID?!
STAND BACK.
WHAT ARE YOU DOING?
GETTING THE FIRE LORD'S ATTENTION.
HWOOOO!

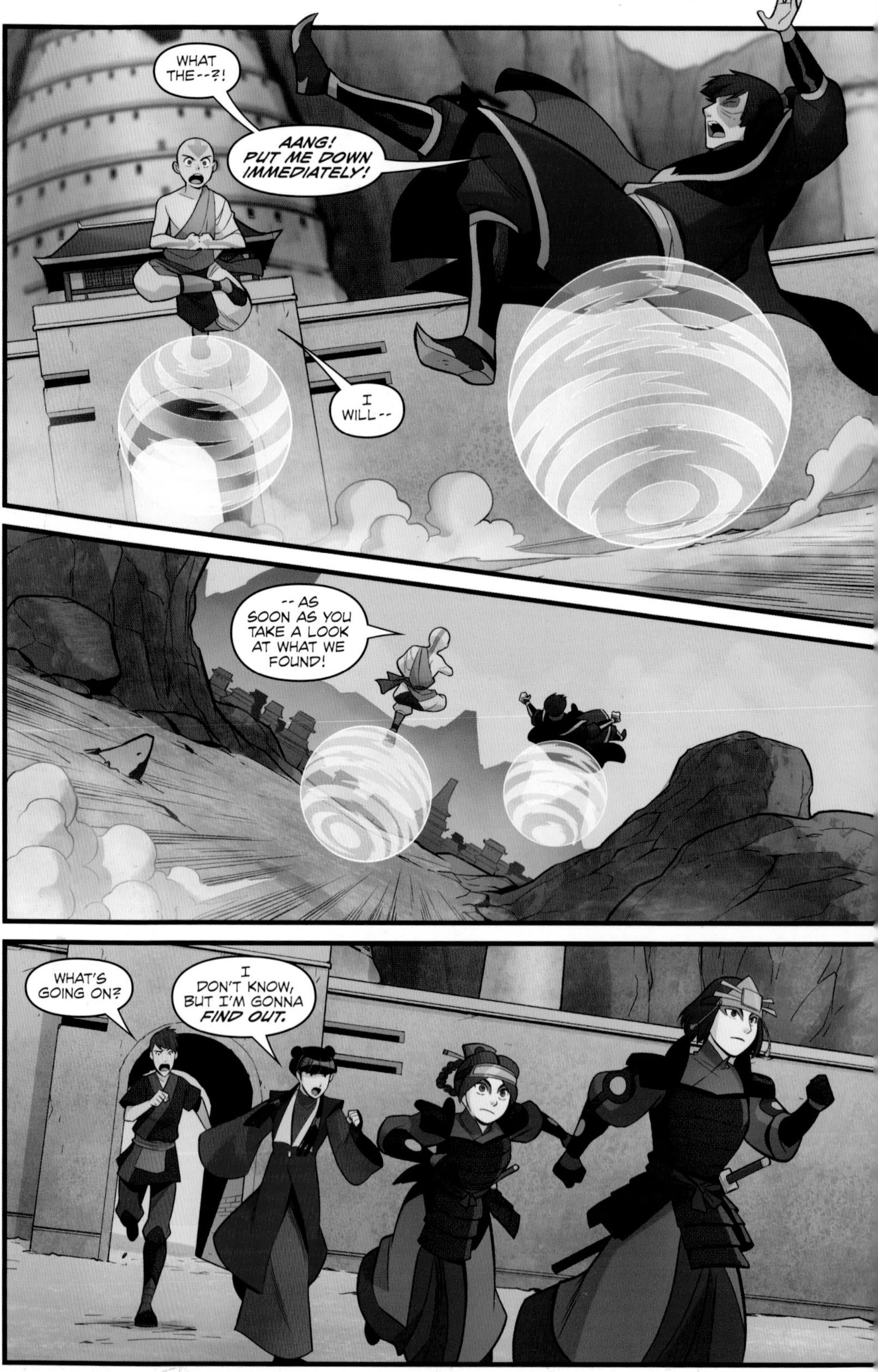
WHAT THE--?!
AANG! PUT ME DOWN IMMEDIATELY!
I WILL--
--AS SOON AS YOU TAKE A LOOK AT WHAT WE FOUND!
WHAT'S GOING ON?
I DON'T KNOW, BUT I'M GONNA FIND OUT.

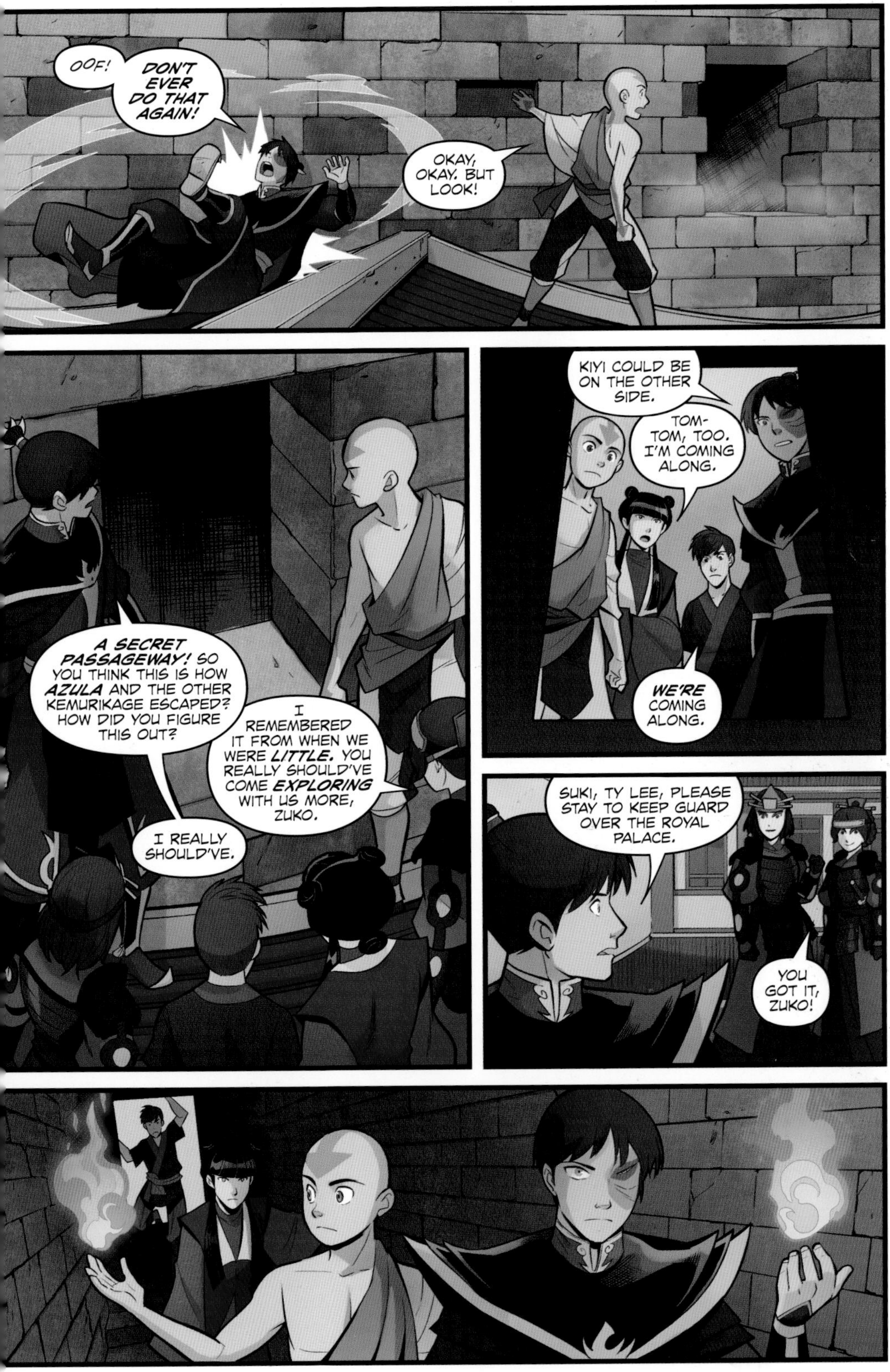
OOF!
DON'T EVER DO THAT AGAIN!
OKAY, OKAY. BUT LOOK!
A SECRET PASSAGEWAY! SO YOU THINK THIS IS HOW AZULA AND THE OTHER KEMURIKAGE ESCAPED? HOW DID YOU FIGURE THIS OUT?
I REMEMBERED IT FROM WHEN WE WERE LITTLE. YOU REALLY SHOULD'VE COME EXPLORING WITH US MORE, ZUKO.
I REALLY SHOULD'VE.
KIYI COULD BE ON THE OTHER SIDE.
TOM-TOM, TOO. I'M COMING ALONG.
WE'RE COMING ALONG.
SUKI, TY LEE, PLEASE STAY TO KEEP GUARD OVER THE ROYAL PALACE.
YOU GOT IT, ZUKO!

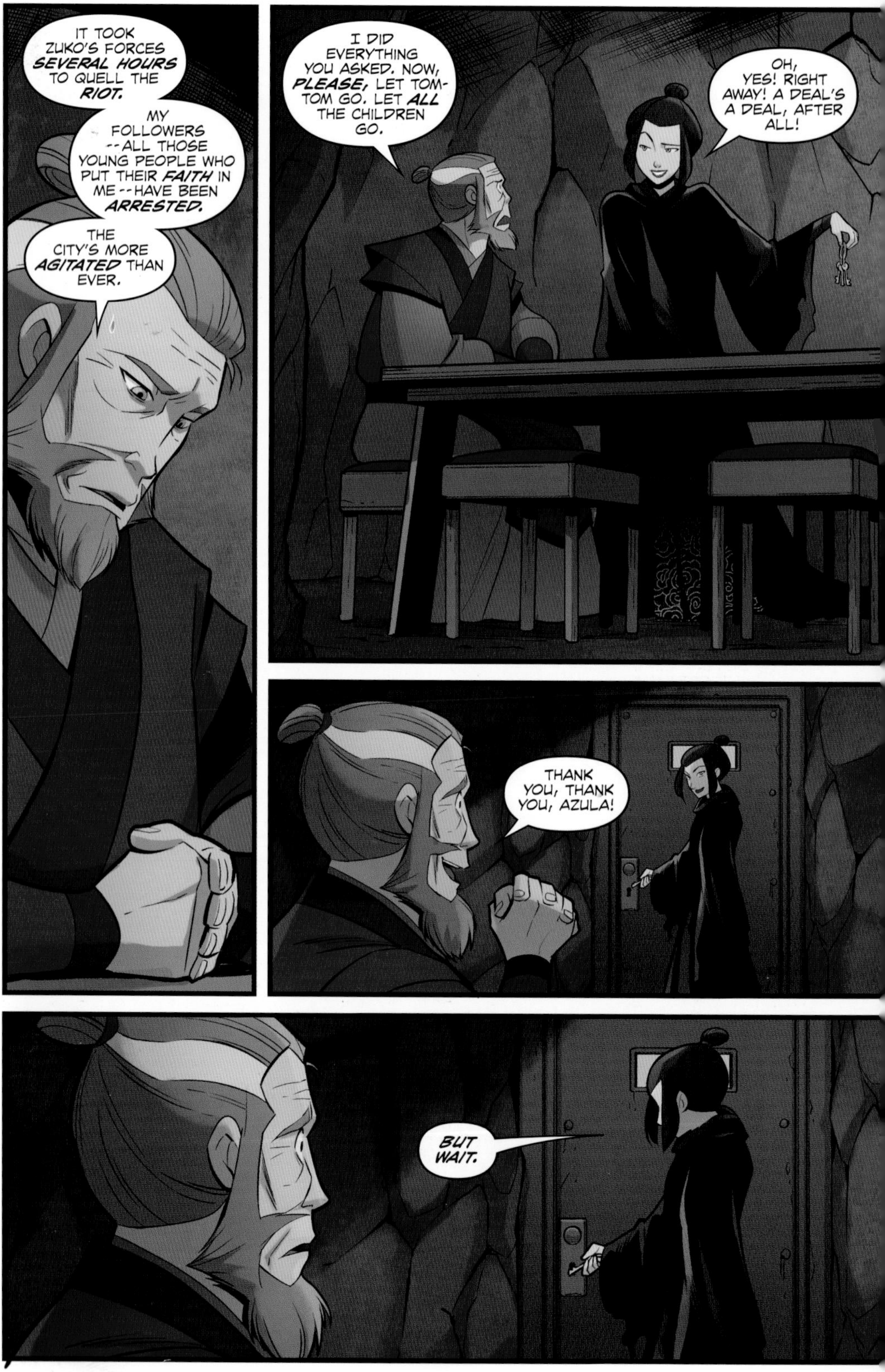
IT TOOK ZUKO'S FORCES SEVERAL HOURS TO QUELL THE RIOT.
MY FOLLOWERS --ALL THOSE YOUNG PEOPLE WHO PUT THEIR FAITH IN ME --HAVE BEEN ARRESTED.
THE CITY'S MORE AGITATED THAN EVER.
I DID EVERYTHING YOU ASKED. NOW, PLEASE, LET TOM-TOM GO. LET ALL THE CHILDREN GO.
OH, YES! RIGHT AWAY! A DEAL'S A DEAL, AFTER ALL!
THANK YOU, THANK YOU, AZULA!
BUT WAIT.

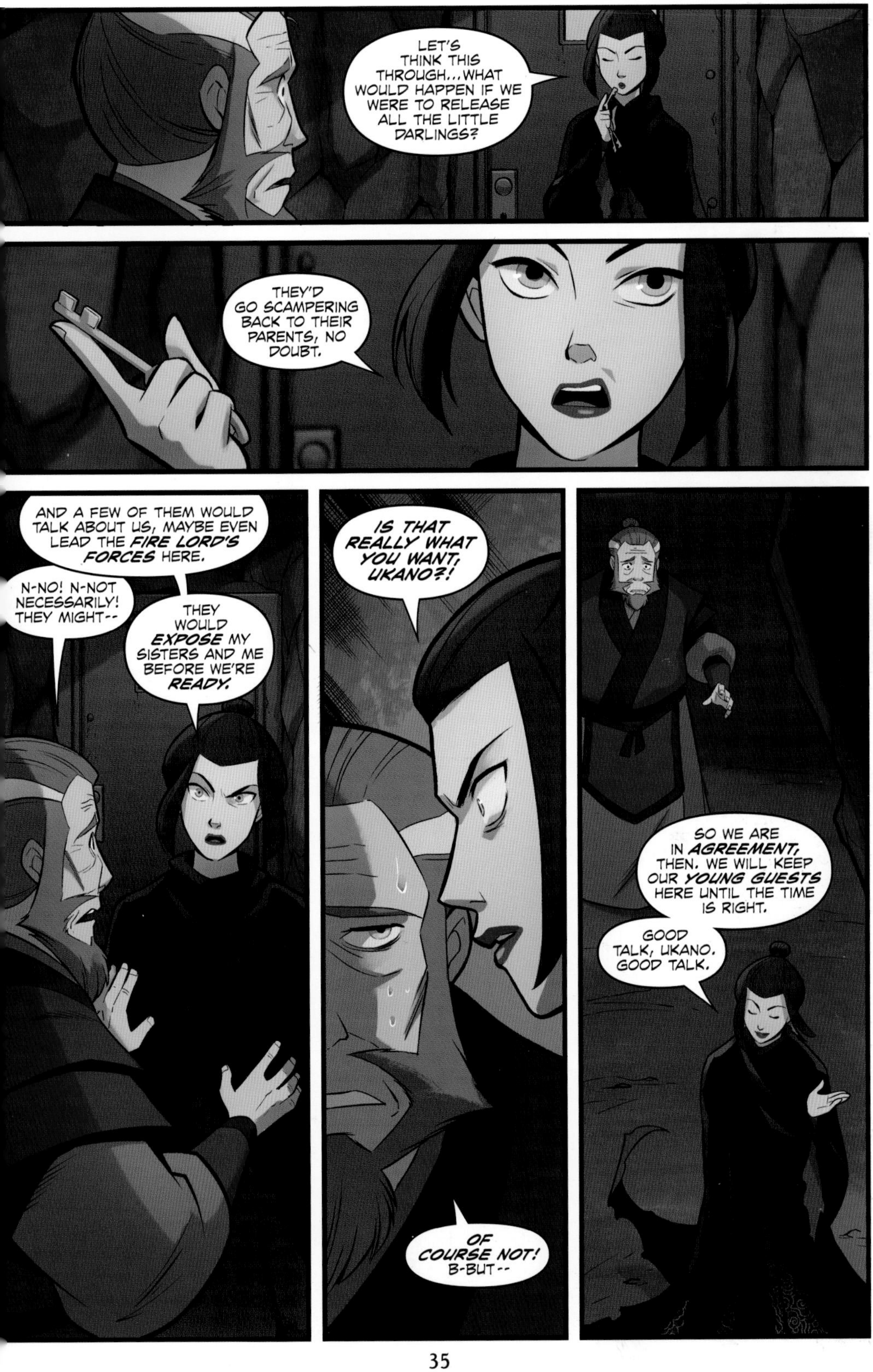
LET'S THINK THIS THROUGH...WHAT WOULD HAPPEN IF WE WERE TO RELEASE ALL THE LITTLE DARLINGS?
THEY'D GO SCAMPERING BACK TO THEIR PARENTS, NO DOUBT.
AND A FEW OF THEM WOULD TALK ABOUT US, MAYBE EVEN LEAD THE FIRE LORD'S FORCES HERE.
N-NO! N-NOT NECESSARILY! THEY MIGHT--
THEY WOULD EXPOSE MY SISTERS AND ME BEFORE WE'RE READY.
IS THAT REALLY WHAT YOU WANT, UKANO?!
OF COURSE NOT! B-BUT--
SO WE ARE IN AGREEMENT, THEN. WE WILL KEEP OUR YOUNG GUESTS HERE UNTIL THE TIME IS RIGHT.
GOOD TALK, UKANO. GOOD TALK.

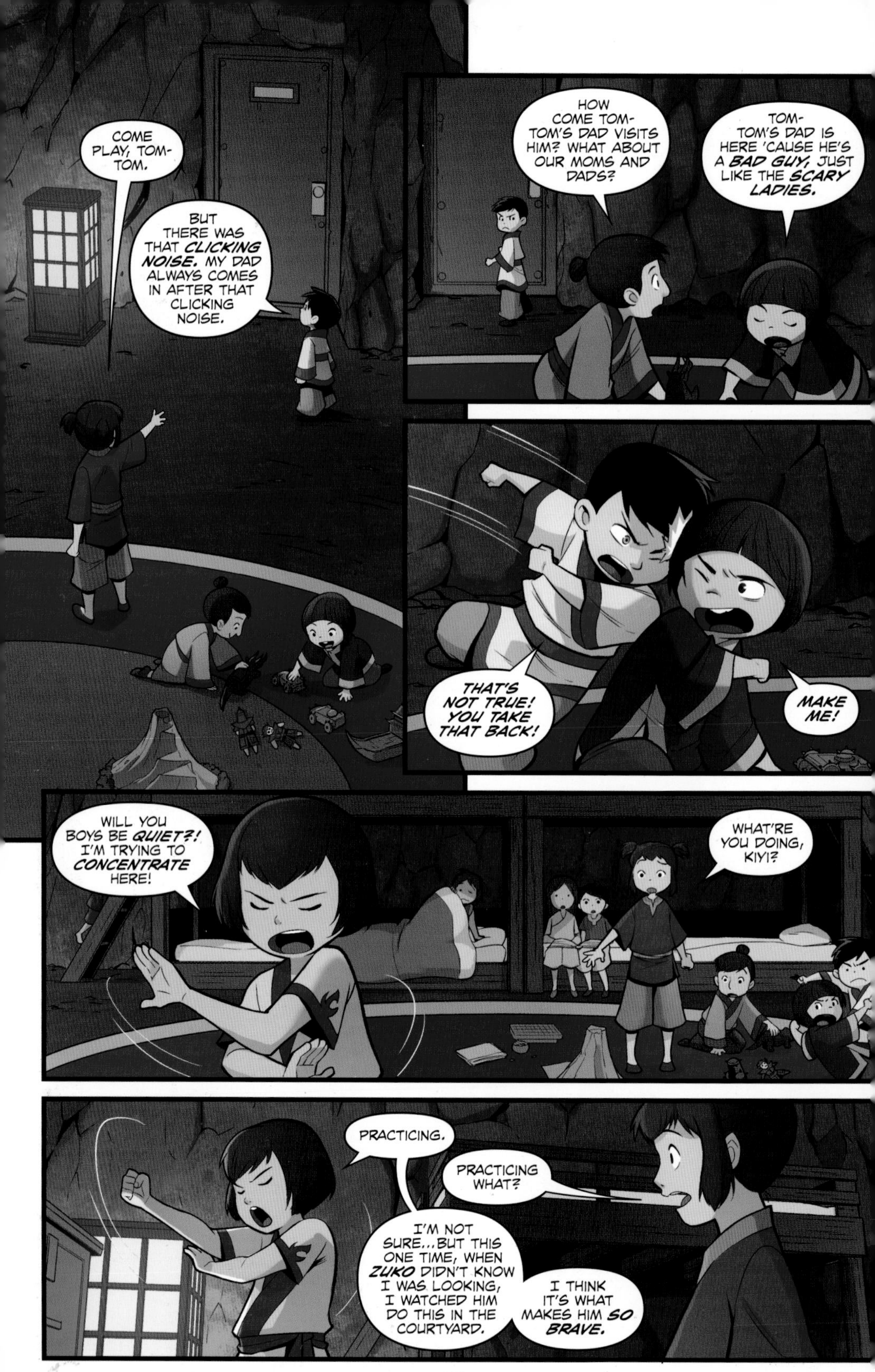
COME PLAY, TOM-TOM.
BUT THERE WAS THAT CLICKING NOISE. MY DAD ALWAYS COMES IN AFTER THAT CLICKING NOISE.
HOW COME TOM-TOM'S DAD VISITS HIM? WHAT ABOUT OUR MOMS AND DADS?
TOM-TOM'S DAD IS HERE 'CAUSE HE'S A BAD GUY, JUST LIKE THE SCARY LADIES.
THAT'S NOT TRUE! YOU TAKE THAT BACK!
MAKE ME!
WILL YOU BOYS BE QUIET?! I'M TRYING TO CONCENTRATE HERE!
WHAT'RE YOU DOING, KIYI?
PRACTICING.
PRACTICING WHAT?
I'M NOT SURE... BUT THIS ONE TIME, WHEN ZUKO DIDN'T KNOW I WAS LOOKING, I WATCHED HIM DO THIS IN THE COURTYARD.
I THINK IT'S WHAT MAKES HIM SO BRAVE.

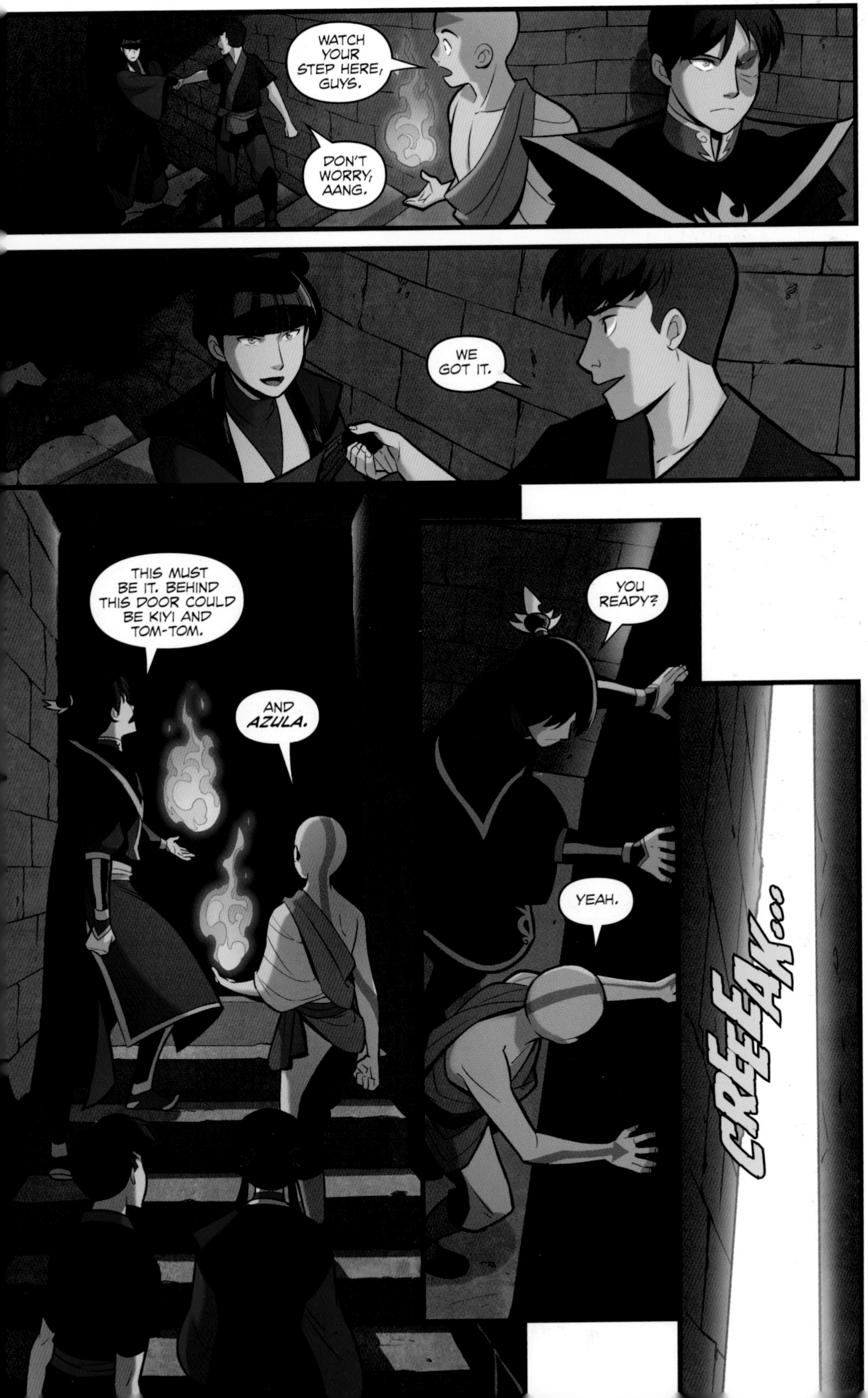
WATCH YOUR STEP HERE, GUYS.
DON'T WORRY, AANG.
WE GOT IT.
THIS MUST BE IT. BEHIND THIS DOOR COULD BE KIYI AND TOM-TOM.
AND *AZULA.*
YOU READY?
YEAH.
CREEEAKooo

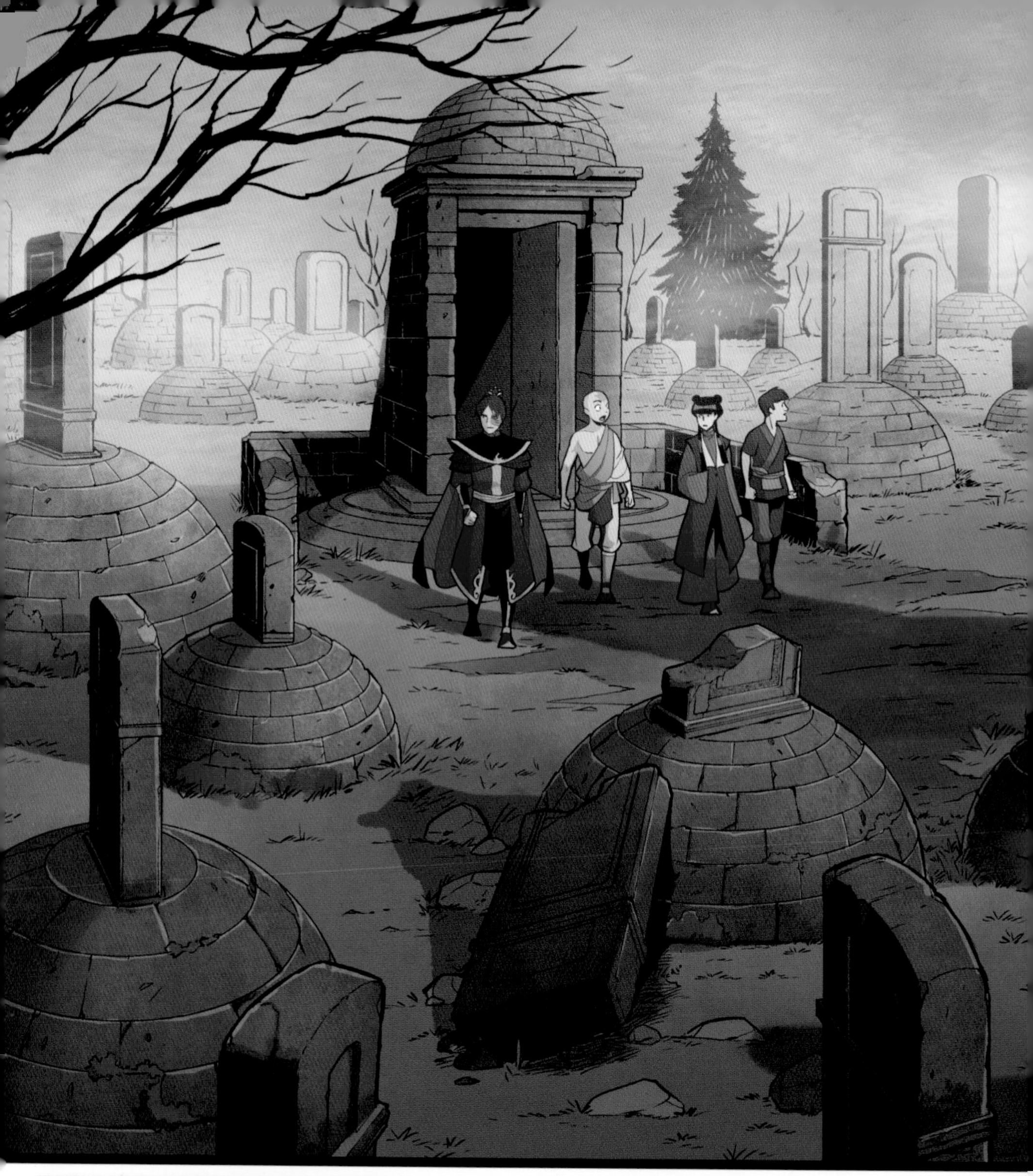

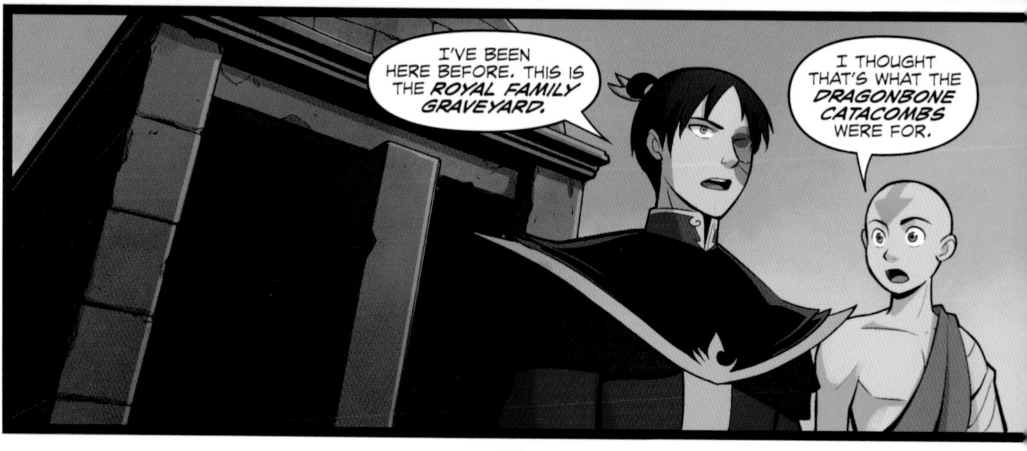
I'VE BEEN HERE BEFORE. THIS IS THE ROYAL FAMILY GRAVEYARD.
I THOUGHT THAT'S WHAT THE DRAGONBONE CATACOMBS WERE FOR.

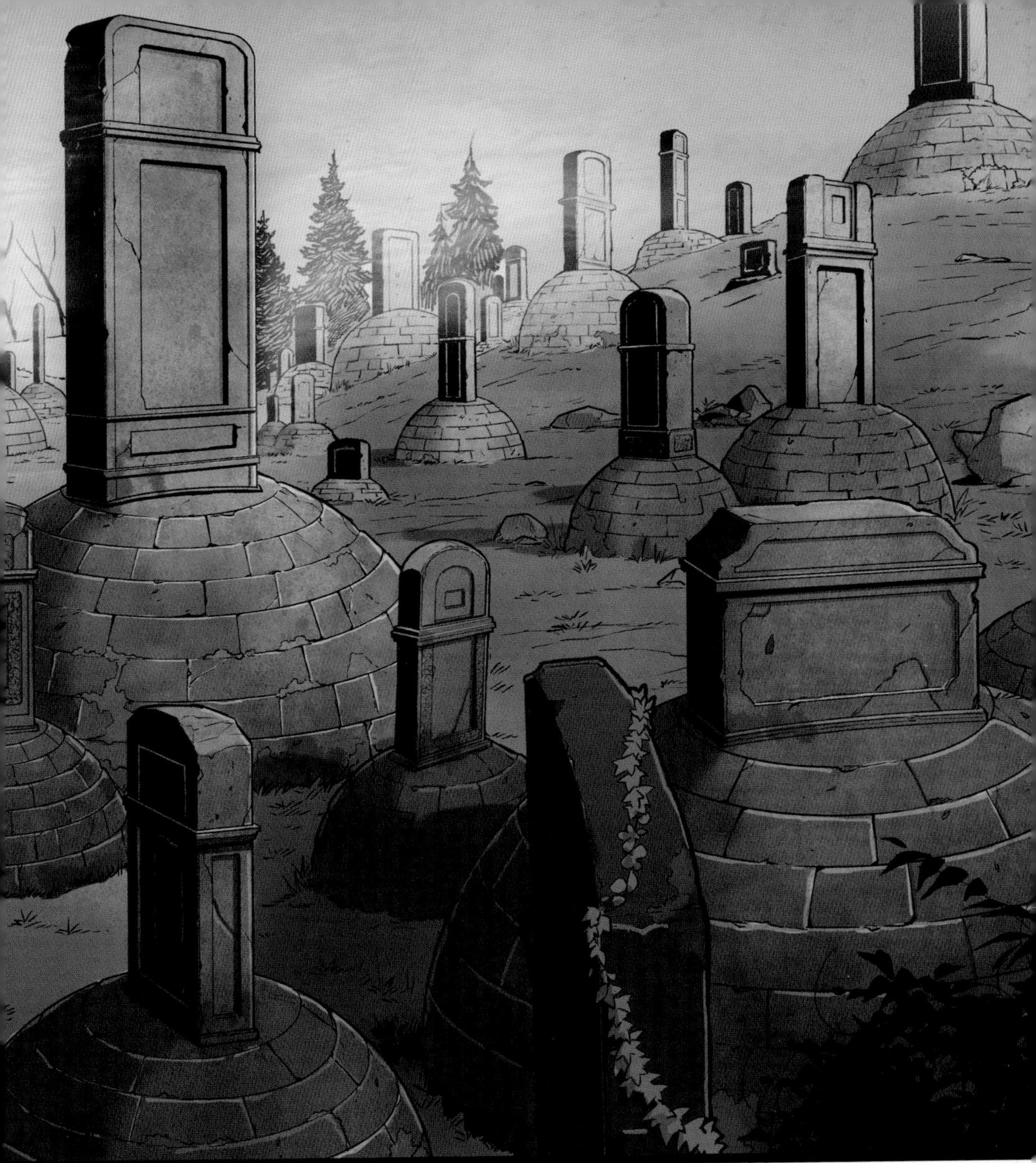

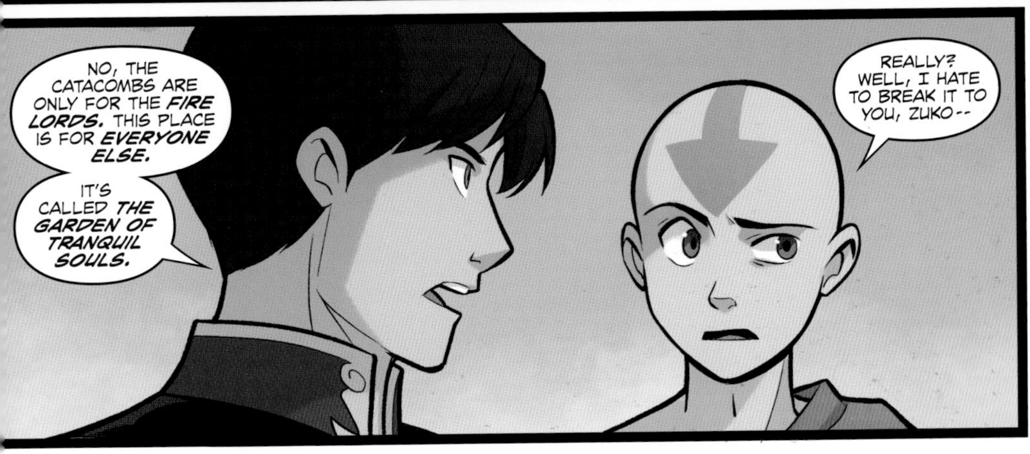
NO, THE CATACOMBS ARE ONLY FOR THE FIRE LORDS. THIS PLACE IS FOR EVERYONE ELSE.
IT'S CALLED THE GARDEN OF TRANQUIL SOULS.
REALLY? WELL, I HATE TO BREAK IT TO YOU, ZUKO--

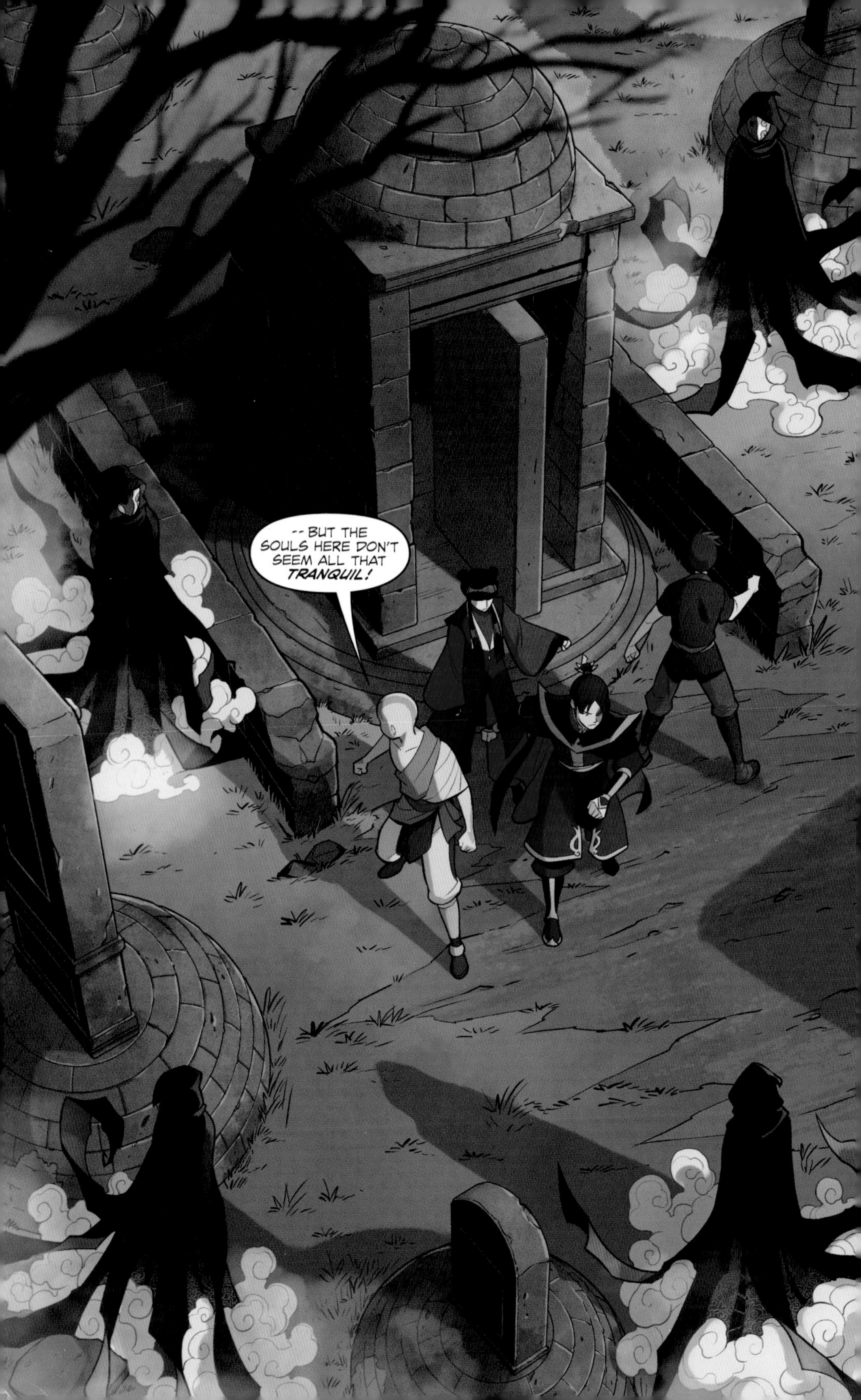
-- BUT THE SOULS HERE DON'T SEEM ALL THAT *TRANQUIL!*

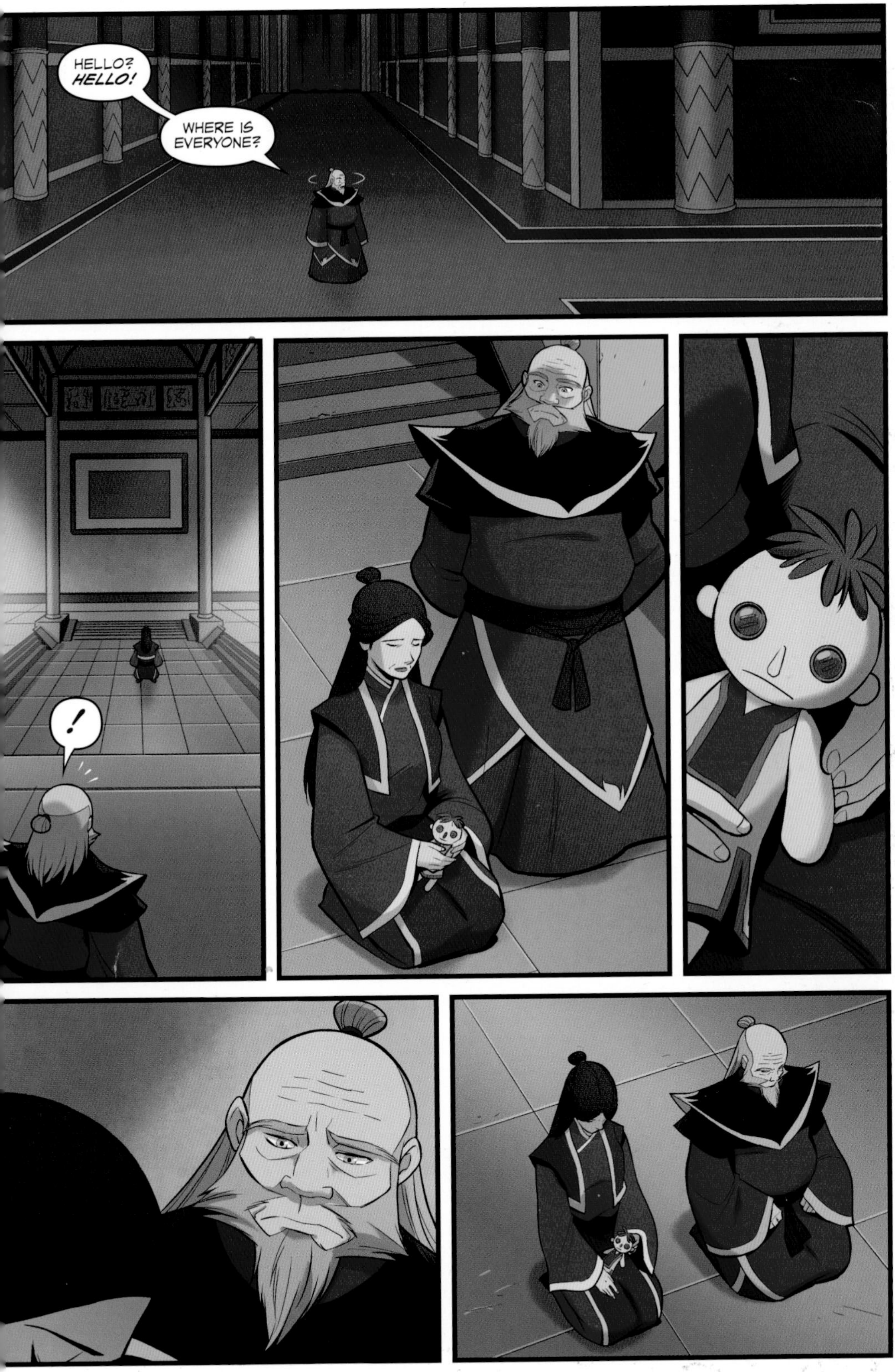
HELLO? HELLO!
WHERE IS EVERYONE?
!

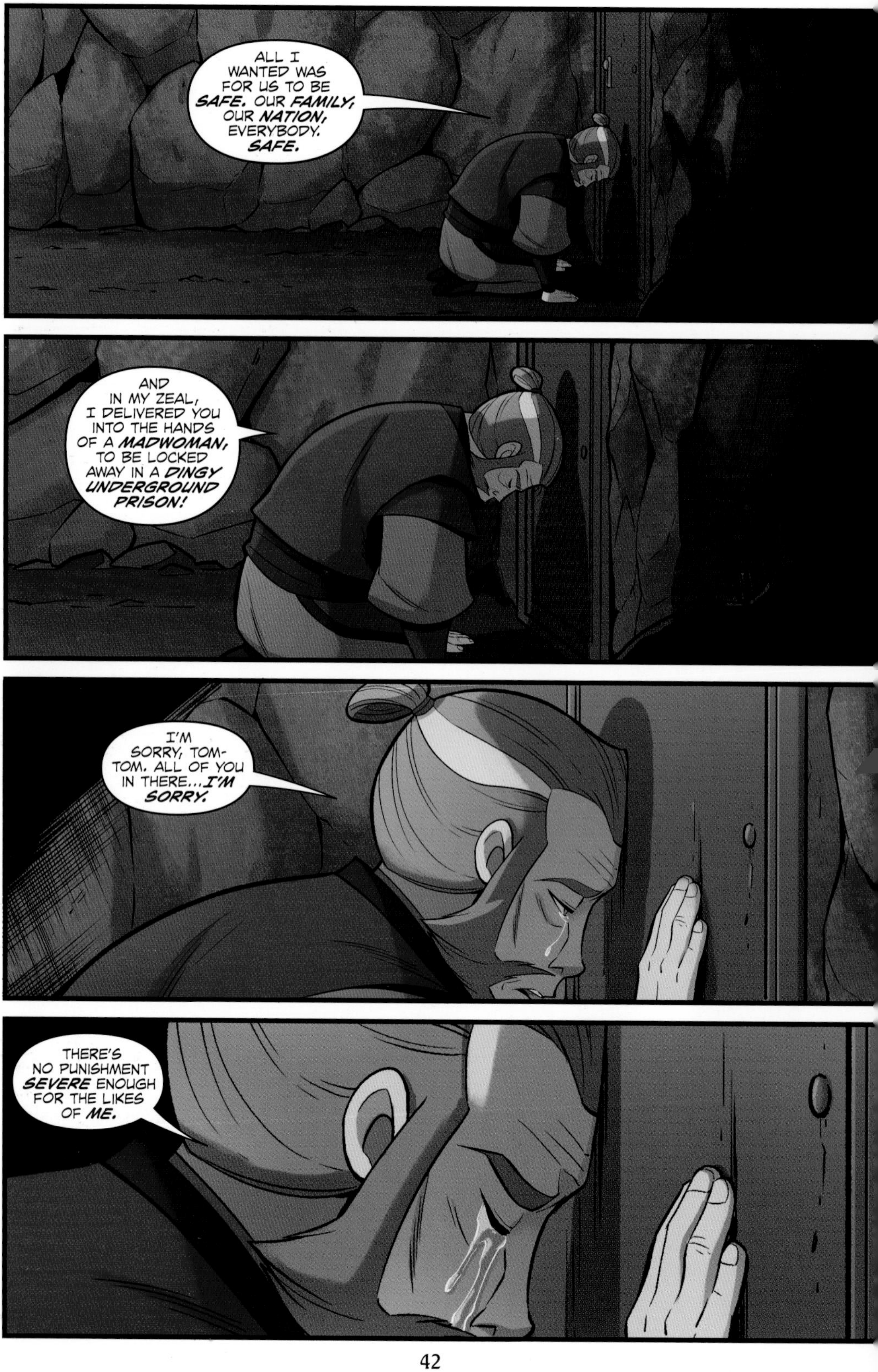
ALL I WANTED WAS FOR US TO BE SAFE. OUR FAMILY, OUR NATION, EVERYBODY. SAFE.
AND IN MY ZEAL, I DELIVERED YOU INTO THE HANDS OF A MADWOMAN, TO BE LOCKED AWAY IN A DINGY UNDERGROUND PRISON!
I'M SORRY, TOM-TOM. ALL OF YOU IN THERE... I'M SORRY.
THERE'S NO PUNISHMENT SEVERE ENOUGH FOR THE LIKES OF ME.

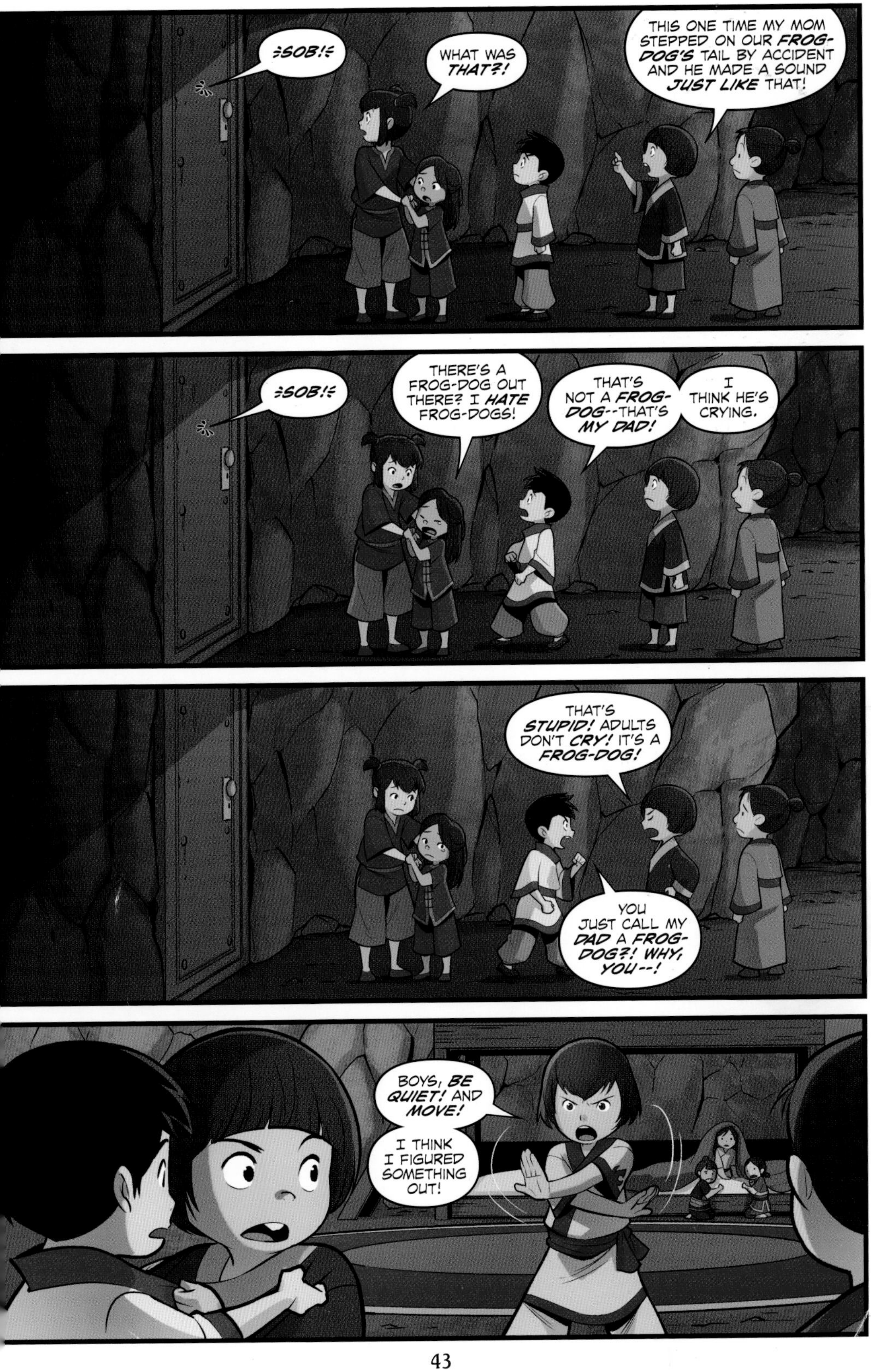
⁑SOB!⁑
WHAT WAS THAT?!
THIS ONE TIME MY MOM STEPPED ON OUR FROG-DOG'S TAIL BY ACCIDENT AND HE MADE A SOUND JUST LIKE THAT!
⁑SOB!⁑
THERE'S A FROG-DOG OUT THERE? I HATE FROG-DOGS!
THAT'S NOT A FROG-DOG--THAT'S MY DAD!
I THINK HE'S CRYING.
THAT'S STUPID! ADULTS DON'T CRY! IT'S A FROG-DOG!
YOU JUST CALL MY DAD A FROG-DOG?! WHY, YOU--!
BOYS, BE QUIET! AND MOVE!
I THINK I FIGURED SOMETHING OUT!

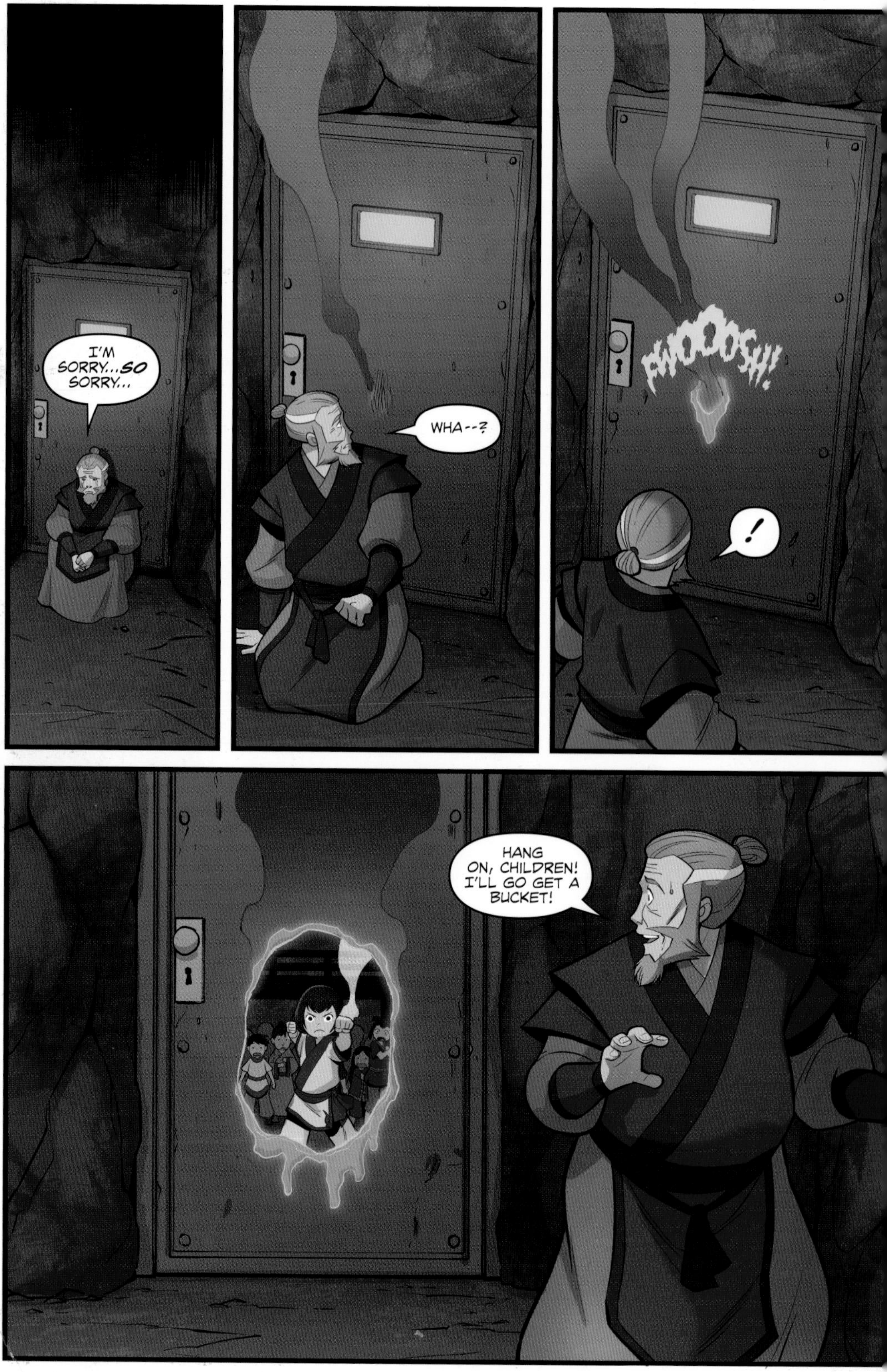
I'M SORRY...SO SORRY...
WHA--?
FWOOOSH!
!
HANG ON, CHILDREN! I'LL GO GET A BUCKET!

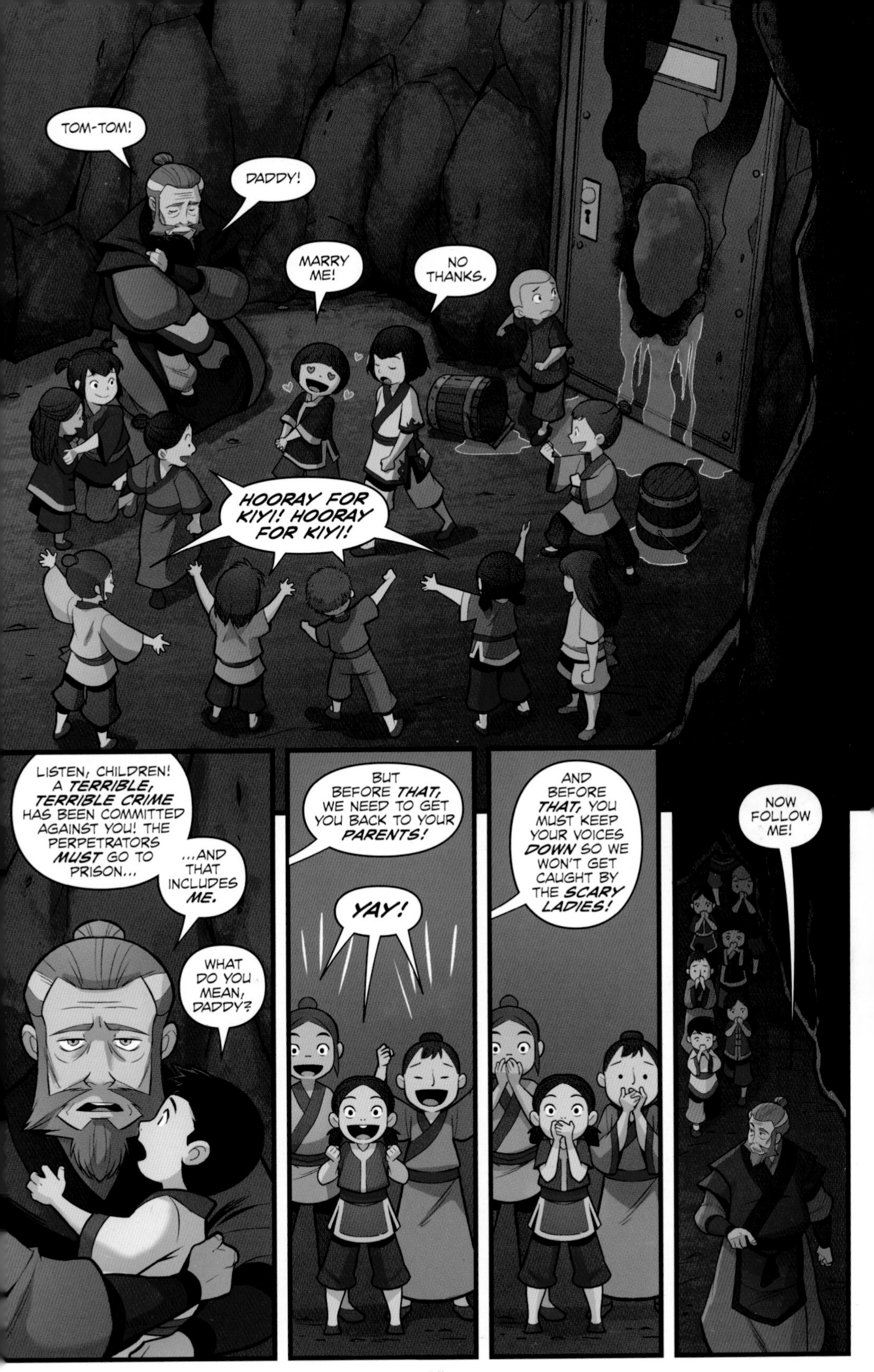
TOM-TOM!
DADDY!
MARRY ME!
NO THANKS.
HOORAY FOR KIYI! HOORAY FOR KIYI!
LISTEN, CHILDREN! A TERRIBLE, TERRIBLE CRIME HAS BEEN COMMITTED AGAINST YOU! THE PERPETRATORS MUST GO TO PRISON...
...AND THAT INCLUDES ME.
WHAT DO YOU MEAN, DADDY?
BUT BEFORE THAT, WE NEED TO GET YOU BACK TO YOUR PARENTS!
YAY!
AND BEFORE THAT, YOU MUST KEEP YOUR VOICES DOWN SO WE WON'T GET CAUGHT BY THE SCARY LADIES!
NOW FOLLOW ME!

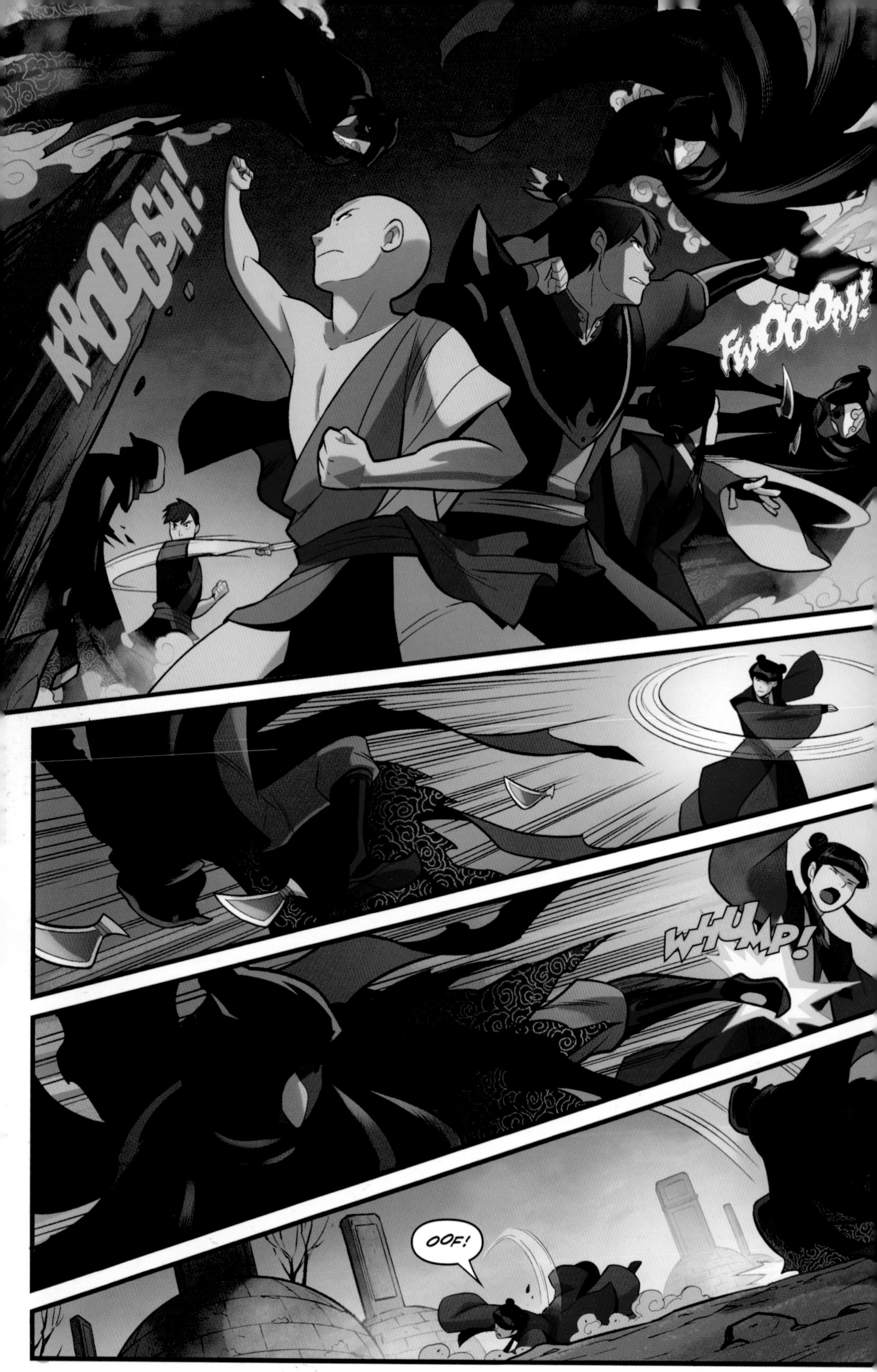
KROOOSH!
FWOOOM!
WHUMP!
OOF!

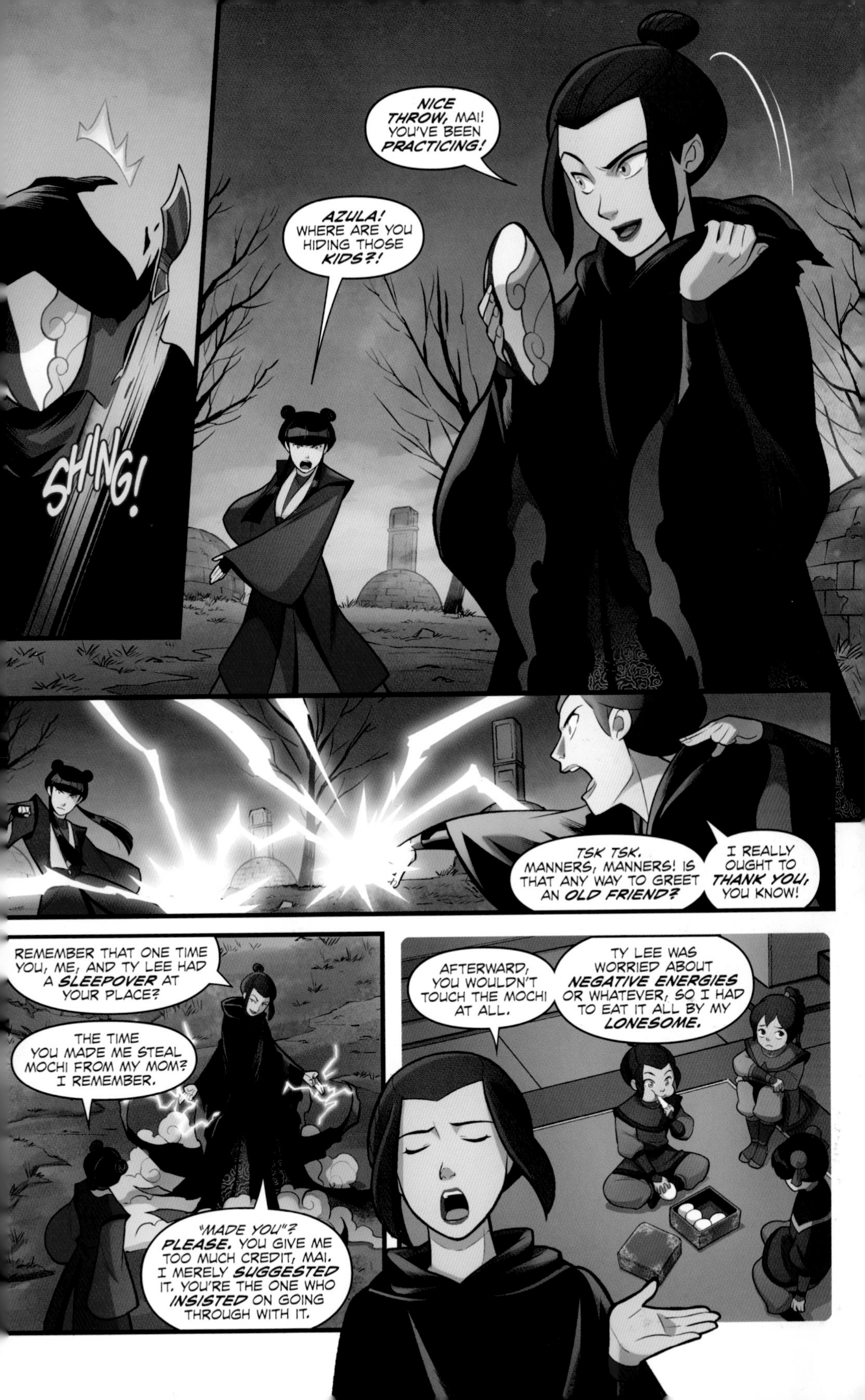

SHING!
NICE THROW, MAI! YOU'VE BEEN PRACTICING!
AZULA! WHERE ARE YOU HIDING THOSE KIDS?!
TSK TSK. MANNERS, MANNERS! IS THAT ANY WAY TO GREET AN OLD FRIEND?
I REALLY OUGHT TO THANK YOU, YOU KNOW!
REMEMBER THAT ONE TIME YOU, ME, AND TY LEE HAD A SLEEPOVER AT YOUR PLACE?
THE TIME YOU MADE ME STEAL MOCHI FROM MY MOM? I REMEMBER.
"MADE YOU"? PLEASE. YOU GIVE ME TOO MUCH CREDIT, MAI. I MERELY SUGGESTED IT. YOU'RE THE ONE WHO INSISTED ON GOING THROUGH WITH IT.
AFTERWARD, YOU WOULDN'T TOUCH THE MOCHI AT ALL.
TY LEE WAS WORRIED ABOUT NEGATIVE ENERGIES OR WHATEVER, SO I HAD TO EAT IT ALL BY MY LONESOME.

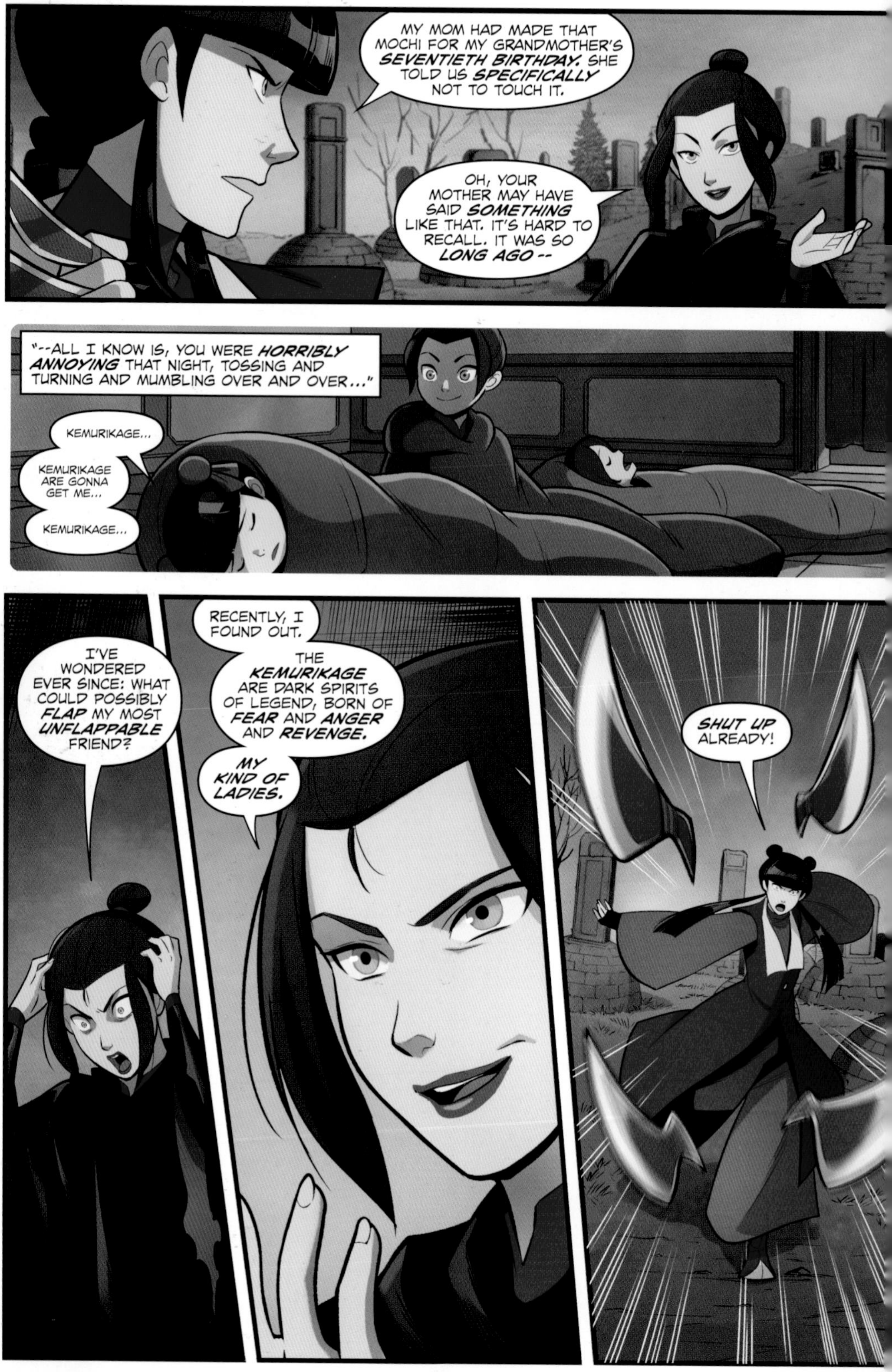
MY MOM HAD MADE THAT MOCHI FOR MY GRANDMOTHER'S SEVENTIETH BIRTHDAY. SHE TOLD US SPECIFICALLY NOT TO TOUCH IT.
OH, YOUR MOTHER MAY HAVE SAID SOMETHING LIKE THAT. IT'S HARD TO RECALL. IT WAS SO LONG AGO --
"--ALL I KNOW IS, YOU WERE HORRIBLY ANNOYING THAT NIGHT, TOSSING AND TURNING AND MUMBLING OVER AND OVER..."
KEMURIKAGE...
KEMURIKAGE ARE GONNA GET ME...
KEMURIKAGE...
I'VE WONDERED EVER SINCE: WHAT COULD POSSIBLY FLAP MY MOST UNFLAPPABLE FRIEND?
RECENTLY, I FOUND OUT.
THE KEMURIKAGE ARE DARK SPIRITS OF LEGEND, BORN OF FEAR AND ANGER AND REVENGE.
MY KIND OF LADIES.
SHUT UP ALREADY!

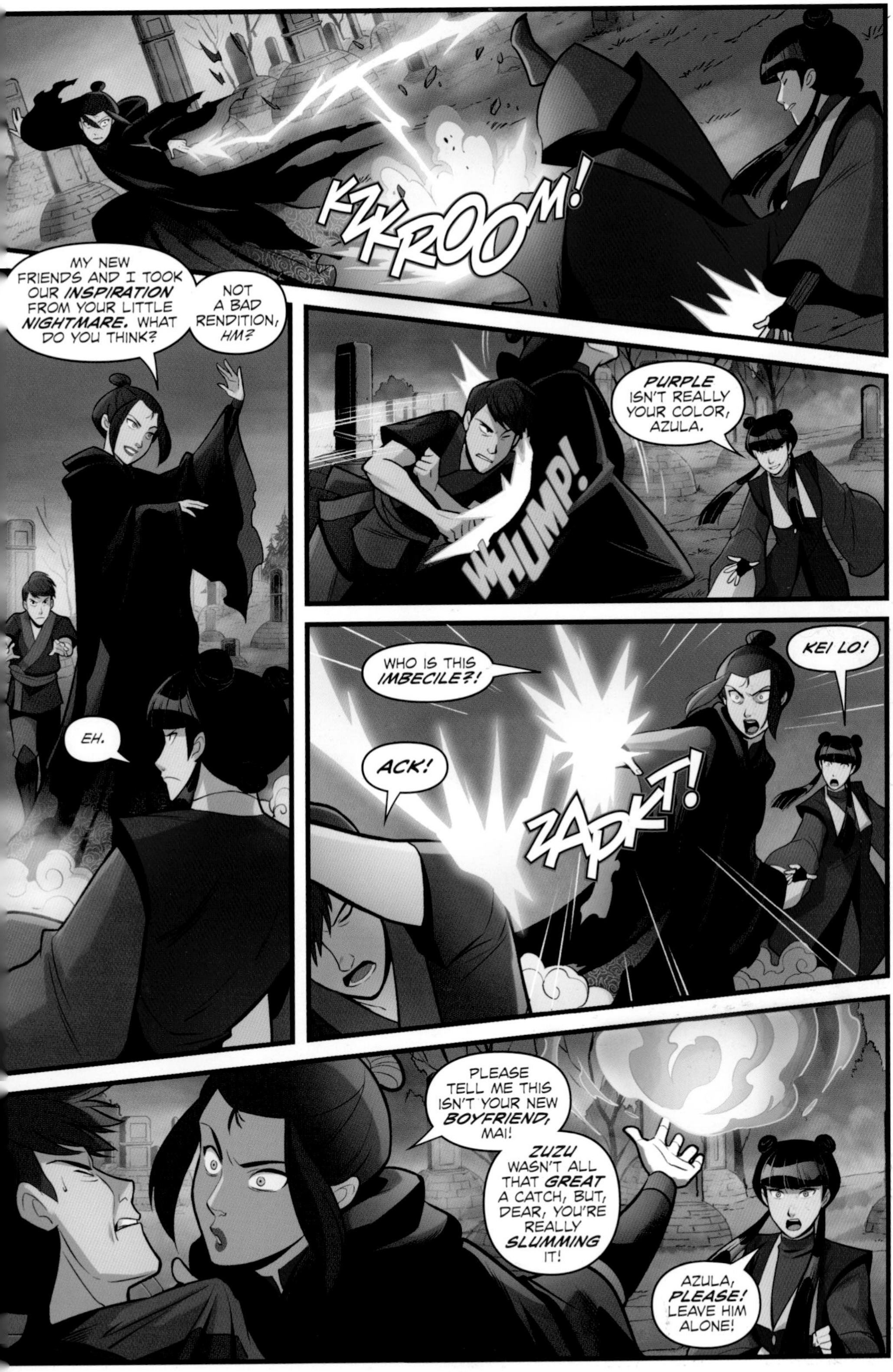
KZKROOM!
MY NEW FRIENDS AND I TOOK OUR INSPIRATION FROM YOUR LITTLE NIGHTMARE. WHAT DO YOU THINK?
NOT A BAD RENDITION, HM?
EH.
PURPLE ISN'T REALLY YOUR COLOR, AZULA.
WHUMP!
WHO IS THIS IMBECILE?!
KEI LO!
ACK!
ZAPKT!
PLEASE TELL ME THIS ISN'T YOUR NEW BOYFRIEND, MAI!
ZUZU WASN'T ALL THAT GREAT A CATCH, BUT, DEAR, YOU'RE REALLY SLUMMING IT!
AZULA, PLEASE! LEAVE HIM ALONE!

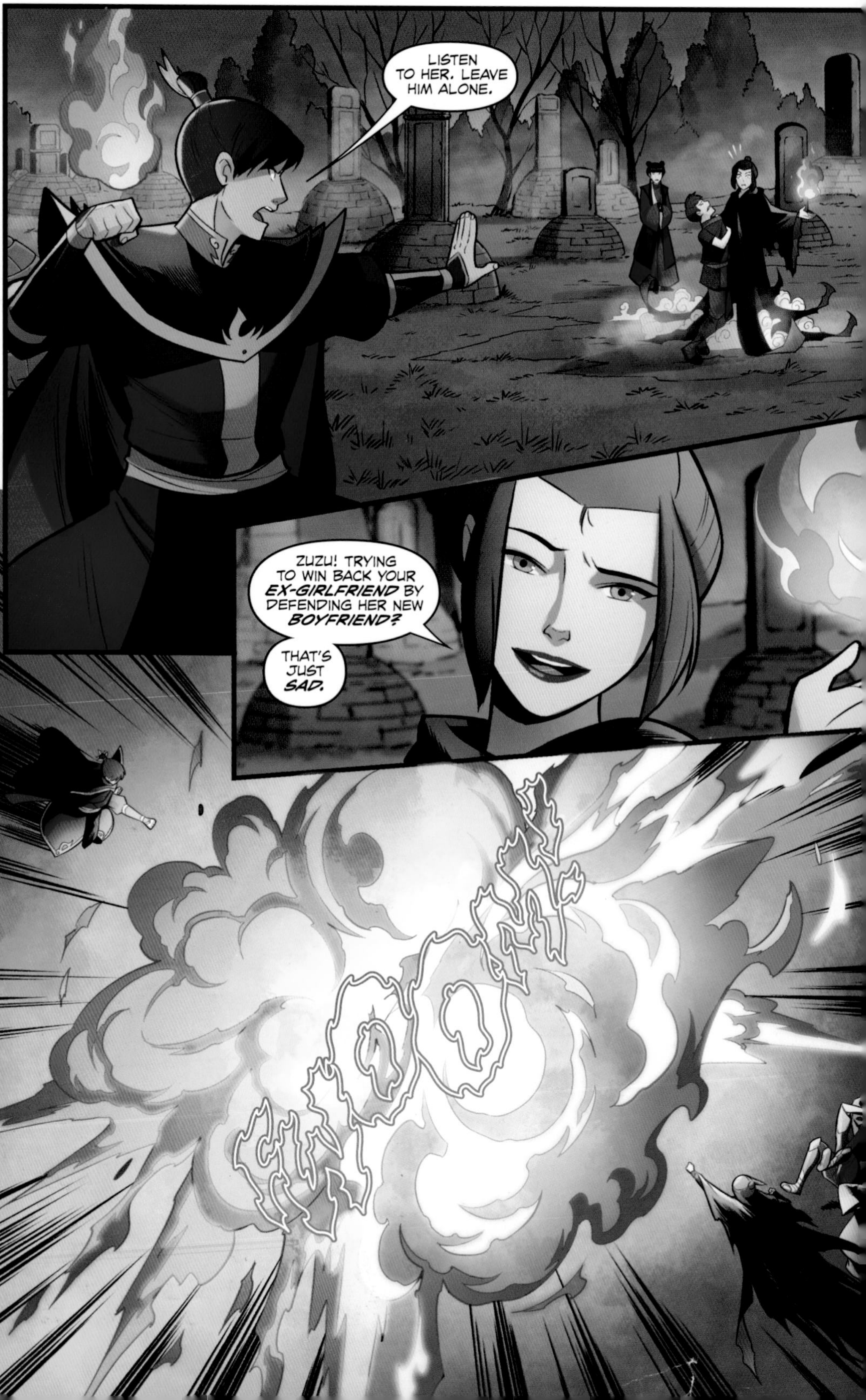
LISTEN TO HER. LEAVE HIM ALONE.
ZUZU! TRYING TO WIN BACK YOUR EX-GIRLFRIEND BY DEFENDING HER NEW BOYFRIEND?
THAT'S JUST SAD.

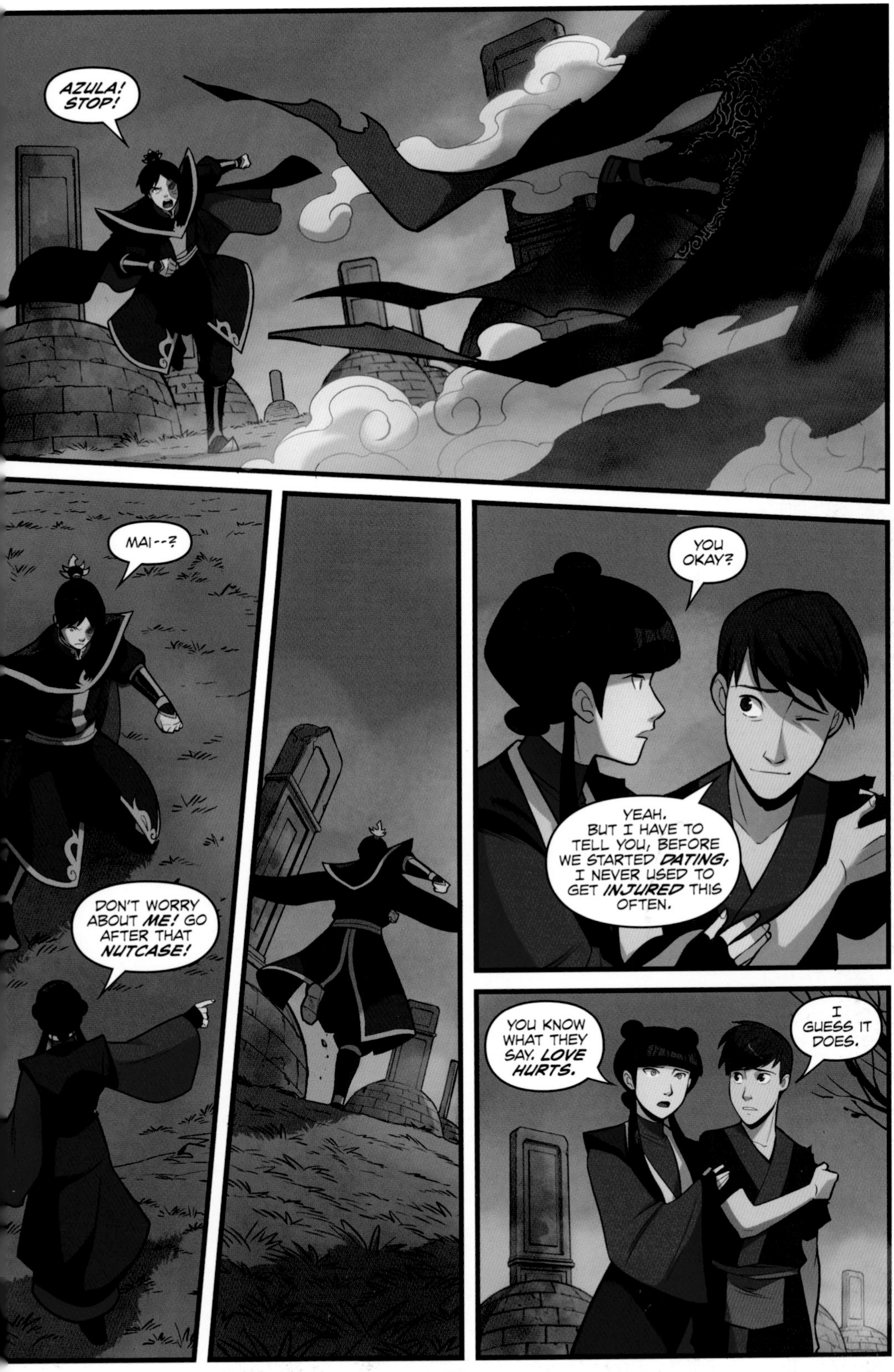
AZULA! STOP!
MAI--?
DON'T WORRY ABOUT ME! GO AFTER THAT NUTCASE!
YOU OKAY?
YEAH. BUT I HAVE TO TELL YOU, BEFORE WE STARTED DATING, I NEVER USED TO GET INJURED THIS OFTEN.
YOU KNOW WHAT THEY SAY. LOVE HURTS.
I GUESS IT DOES.

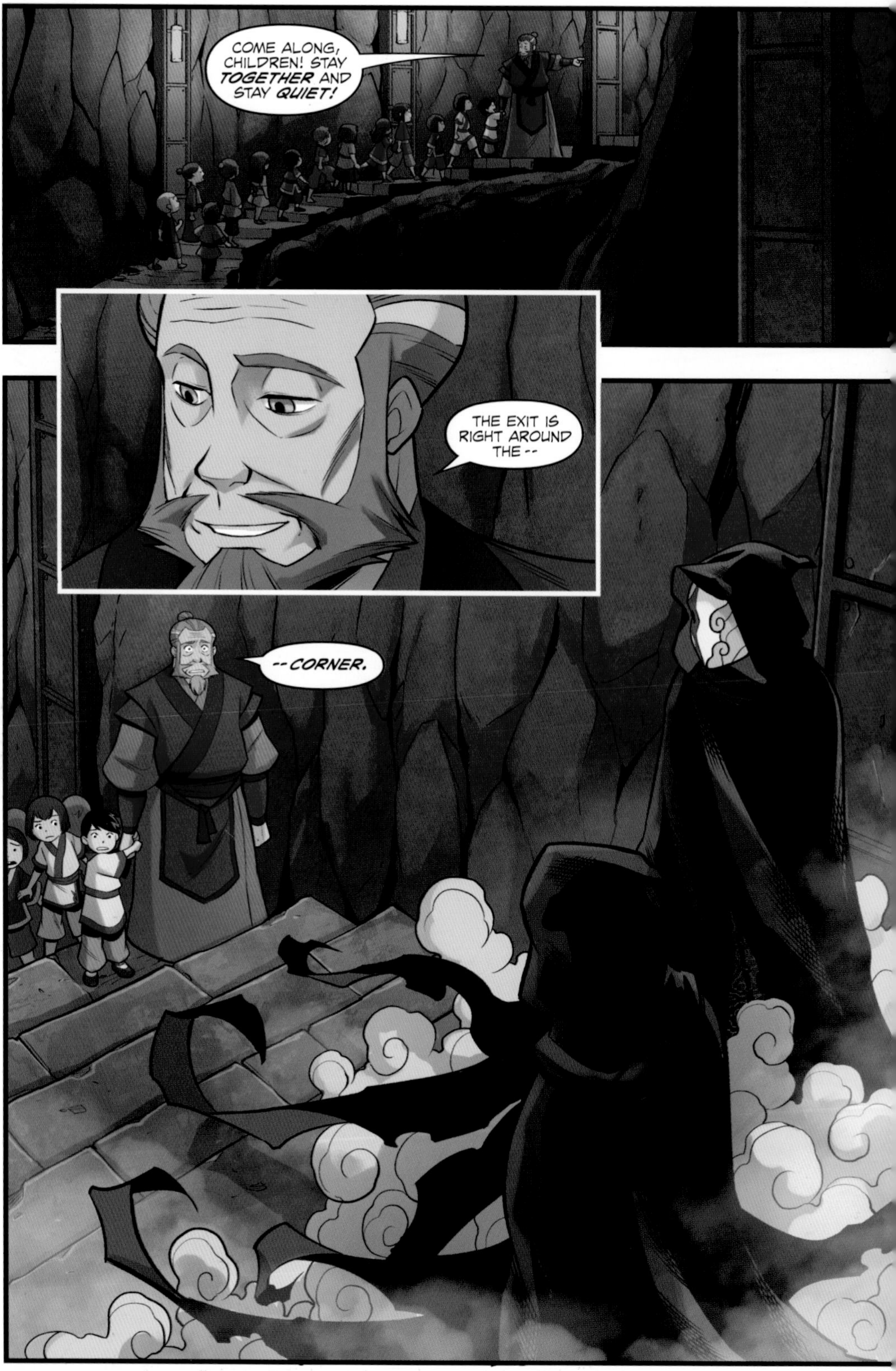
COME ALONG, CHILDREN! STAY TOGETHER AND STAY QUIET!
THE EXIT IS RIGHT AROUND THE --
--CORNER.

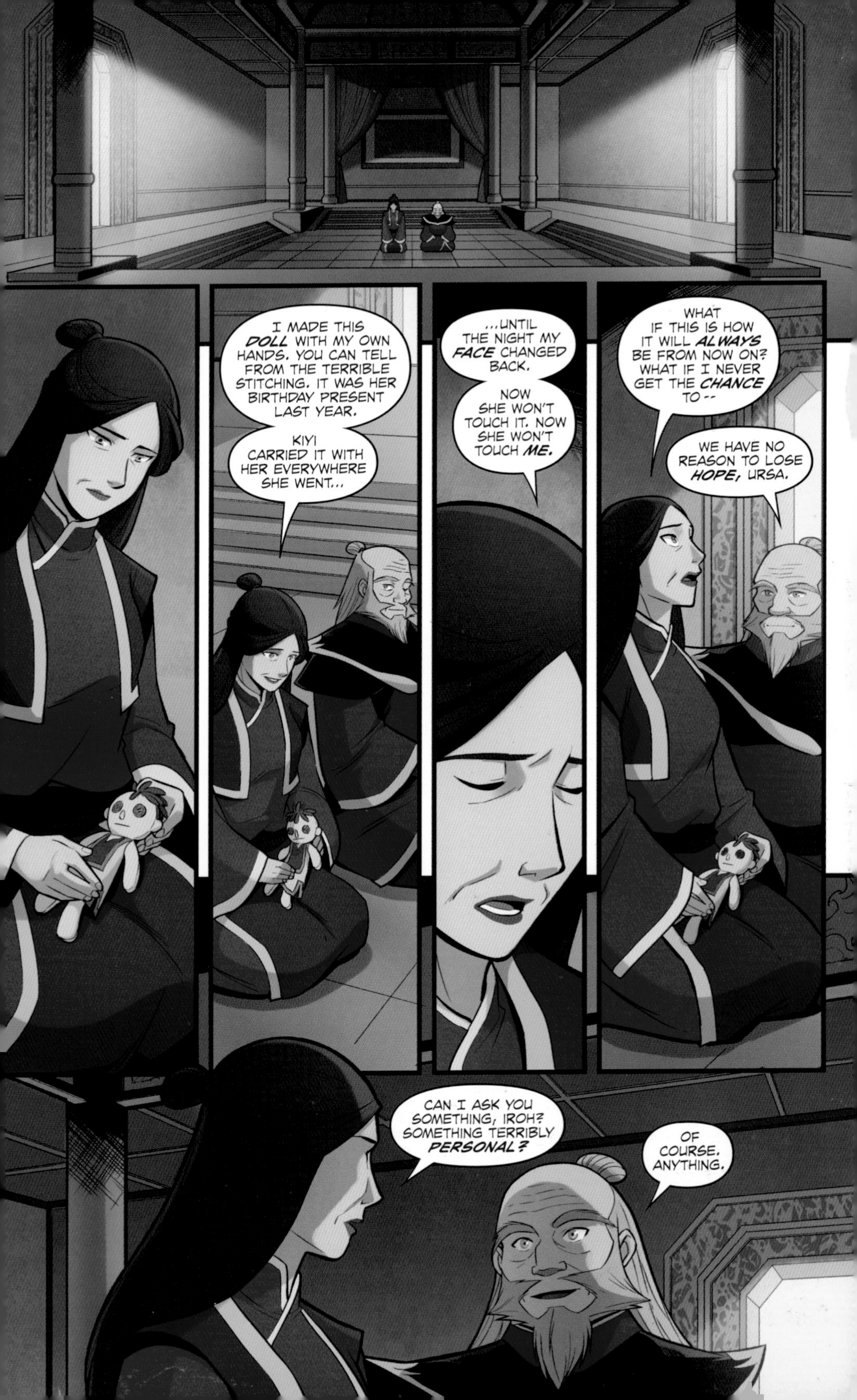
I MADE THIS DOLL WITH MY OWN HANDS. YOU CAN TELL FROM THE TERRIBLE STITCHING. IT WAS HER BIRTHDAY PRESENT LAST YEAR.
KIYI CARRIED IT WITH HER EVERYWHERE SHE WENT...
...UNTIL THE NIGHT MY FACE CHANGED BACK.
NOW SHE WON'T TOUCH IT. NOW SHE WON'T TOUCH ME.
WHAT IF THIS IS HOW IT WILL ALWAYS BE FROM NOW ON? WHAT IF I NEVER GET THE CHANCE TO --
WE HAVE NO REASON TO LOSE HOPE, URSA.
CAN I ASK YOU SOMETHING, IROH? SOMETHING TERRIBLY PERSONAL?
OF COURSE. ANYTHING.

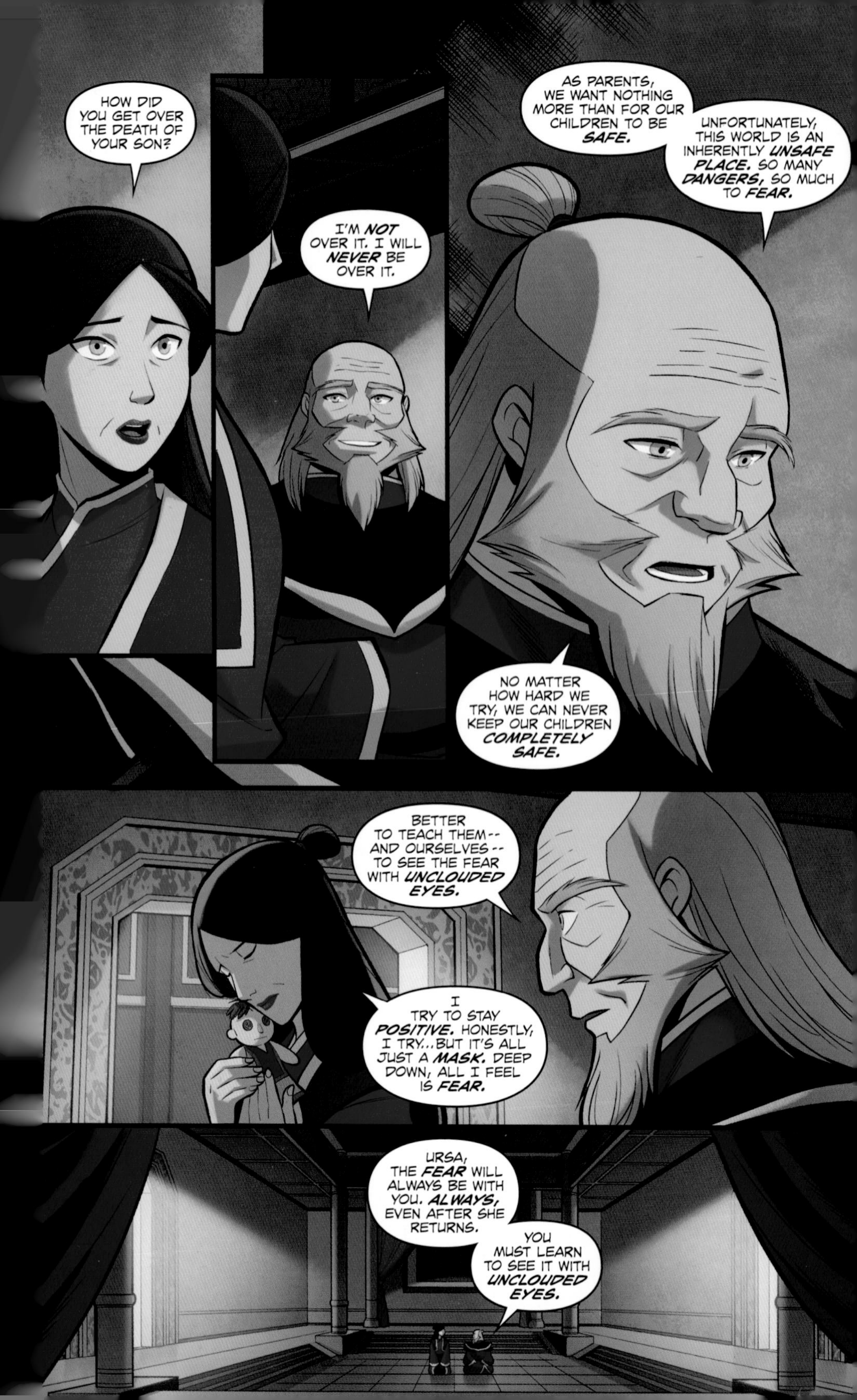
HOW DID YOU GET OVER THE DEATH OF YOUR SON?
I'M NOT OVER IT. I WILL NEVER BE OVER IT.
AS PARENTS, WE WANT NOTHING MORE THAN FOR OUR CHILDREN TO BE SAFE.
UNFORTUNATELY, THIS WORLD IS AN INHERENTLY UNSAFE PLACE. SO MANY DANGERS, SO MUCH TO FEAR.
NO MATTER HOW HARD WE TRY, WE CAN NEVER KEEP OUR CHILDREN COMPLETELY SAFE.
BETTER TO TEACH THEM-- AND OURSELVES-- TO SEE THE FEAR WITH UNCLOUDED EYES.
I TRY TO STAY POSITIVE. HONESTLY, I TRY...BUT IT'S ALL JUST A MASK. DEEP DOWN, ALL I FEEL IS FEAR.
URSA, THE FEAR WILL ALWAYS BE WITH YOU. ALWAYS, EVEN AFTER SHE RETURNS.
YOU MUST LEARN TO SEE IT WITH UNCLOUDED EYES.

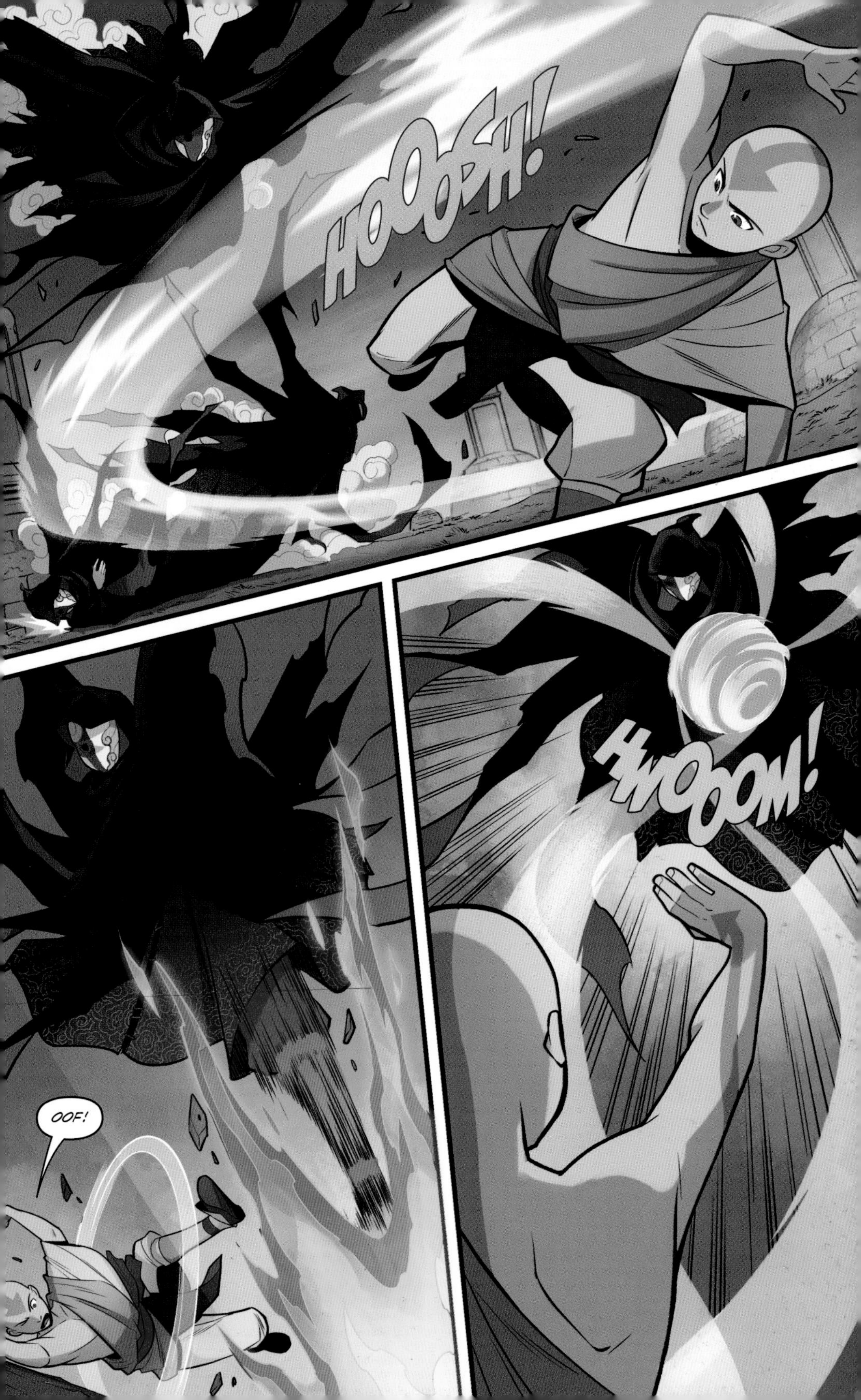
HOOOSH!
HWOOOM!
OOF!

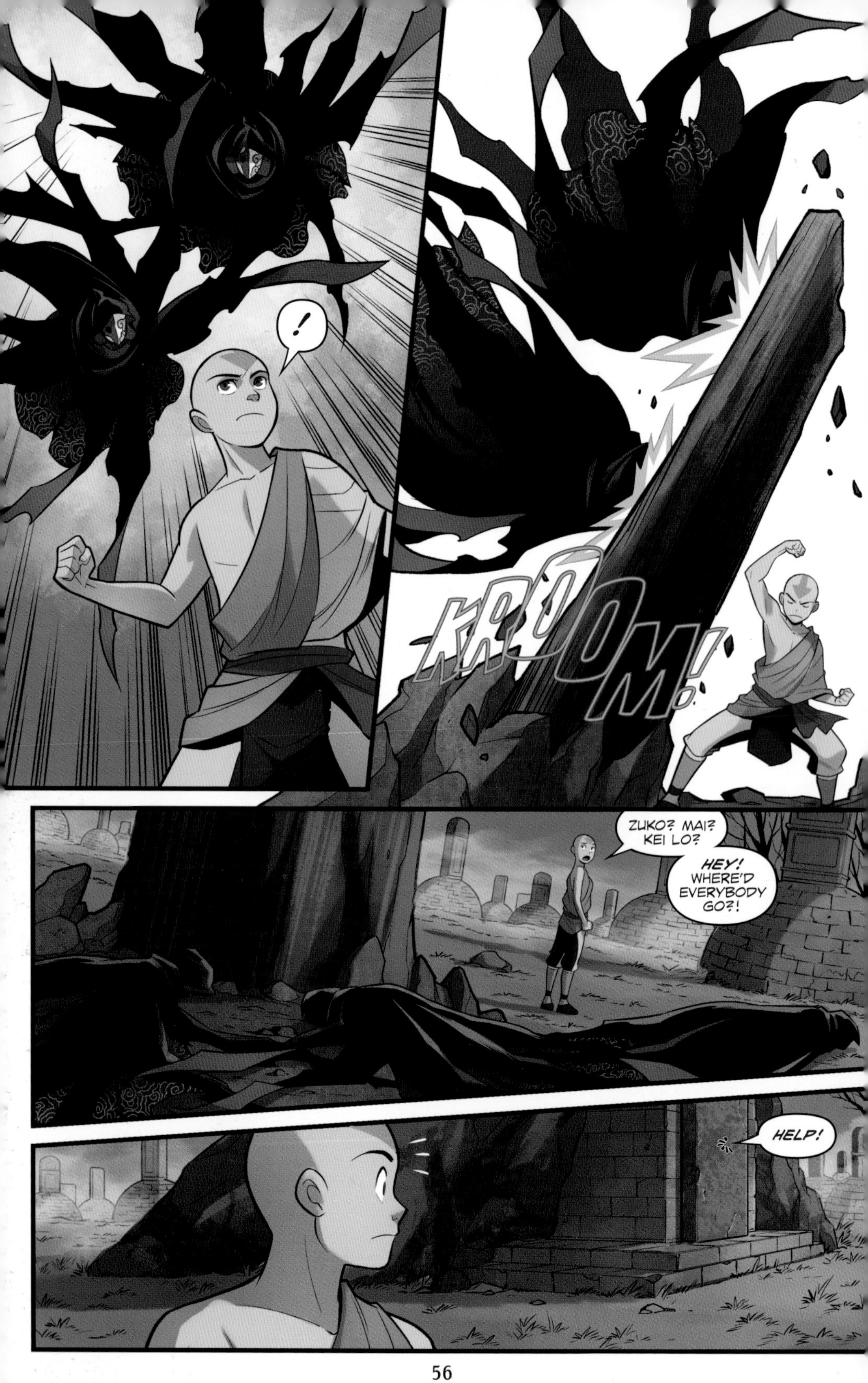
!
KROOOM!
ZUKO? MAI? KEI LO?
HEY! WHERE'D EVERYBODY GO?!
HELP!

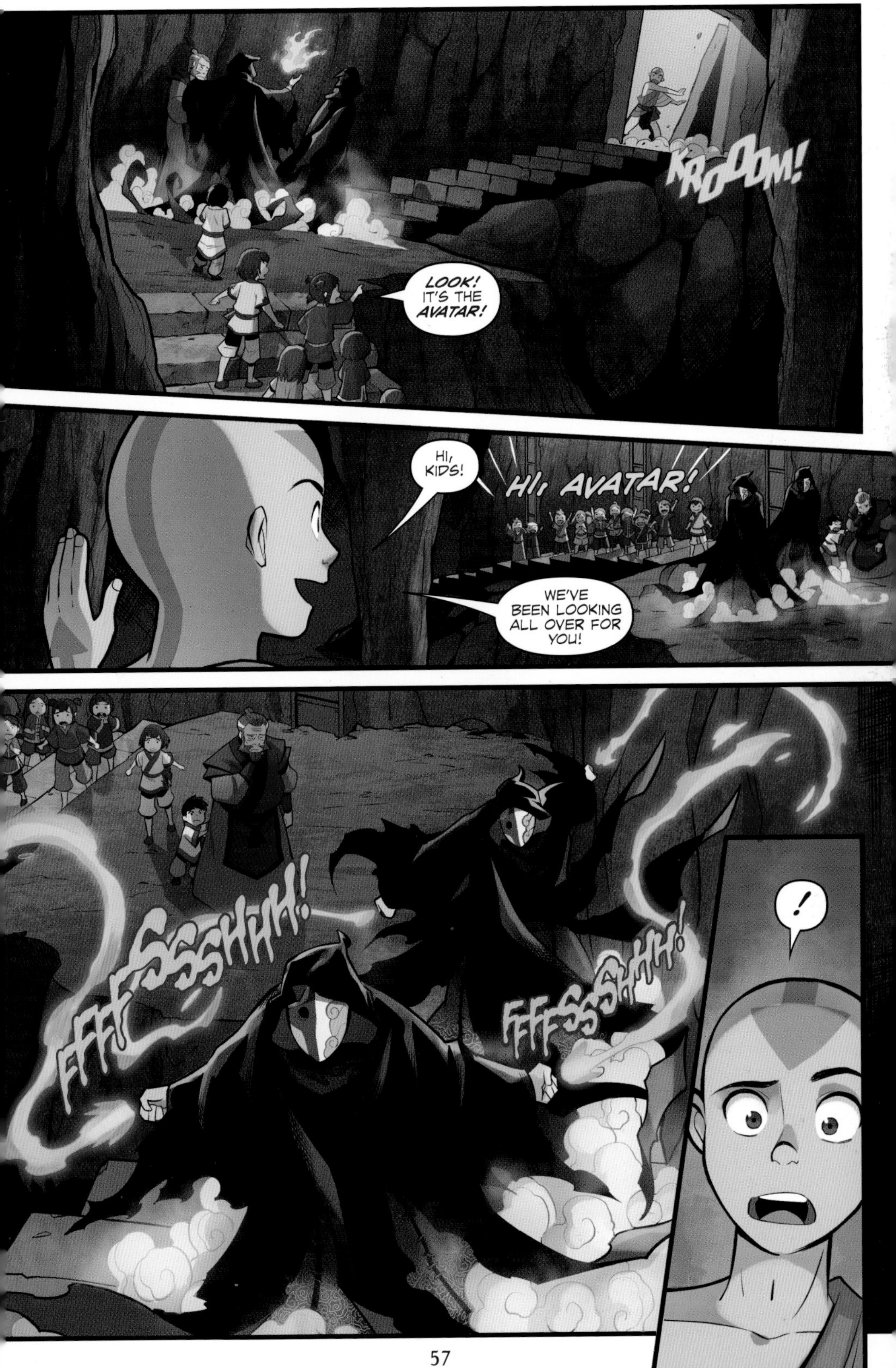
KROOOM!
LOOK! IT'S THE AVATAR!
HI, KIDS!
HI, AVATAR!
WE'VE BEEN LOOKING ALL OVER FOR YOU!
FFFSSSHHH!
FFFFSSSHHH!
!

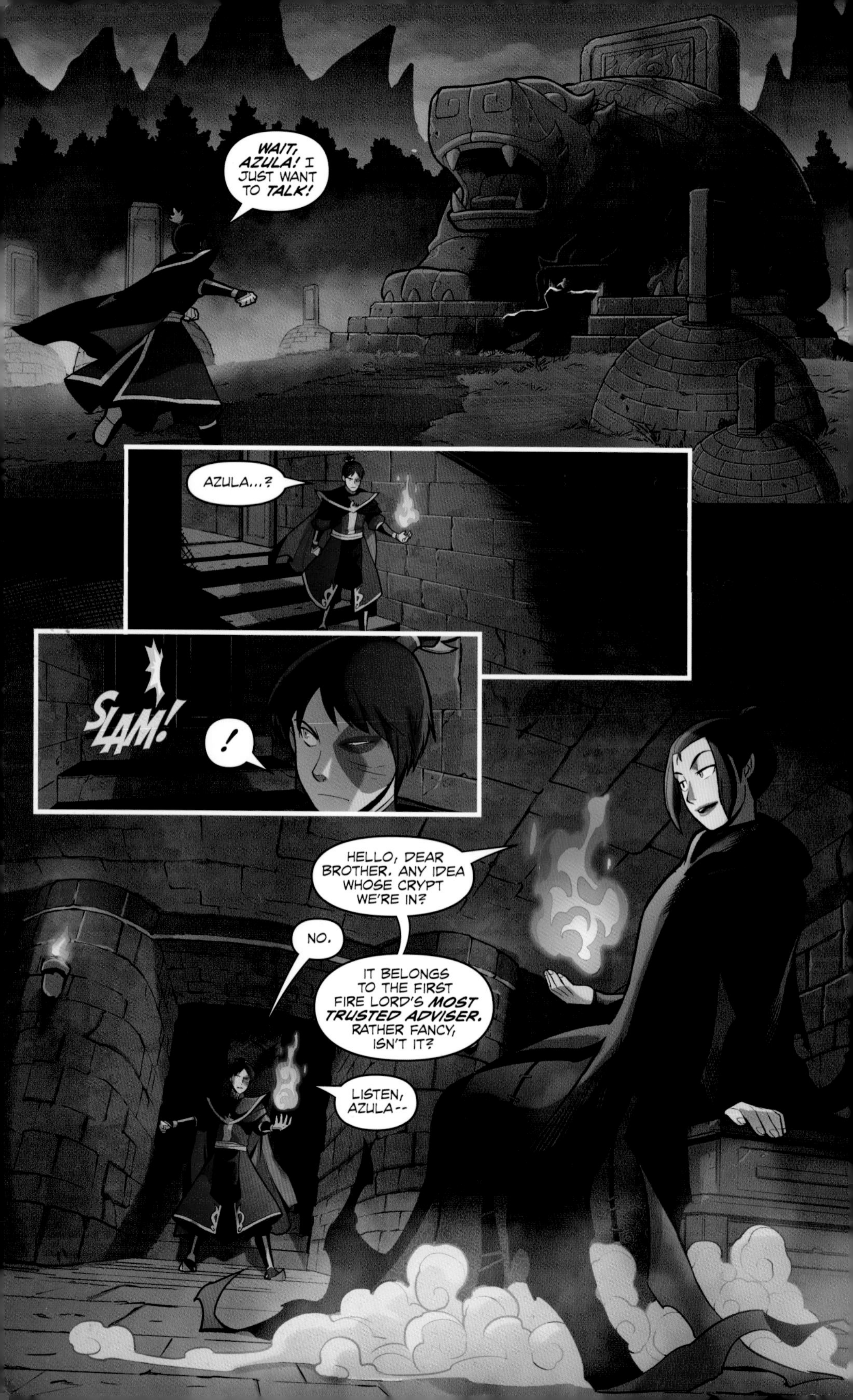
WAIT, AZULA! I JUST WANT TO TALK!
AZULA...?
SLAM!
!
HELLO, DEAR BROTHER. ANY IDEA WHOSE CRYPT WE'RE IN?
NO.
IT BELONGS TO THE FIRST FIRE LORD'S MOST TRUSTED ADVISER. RATHER FANCY, ISN'T IT?
LISTEN, AZULA--

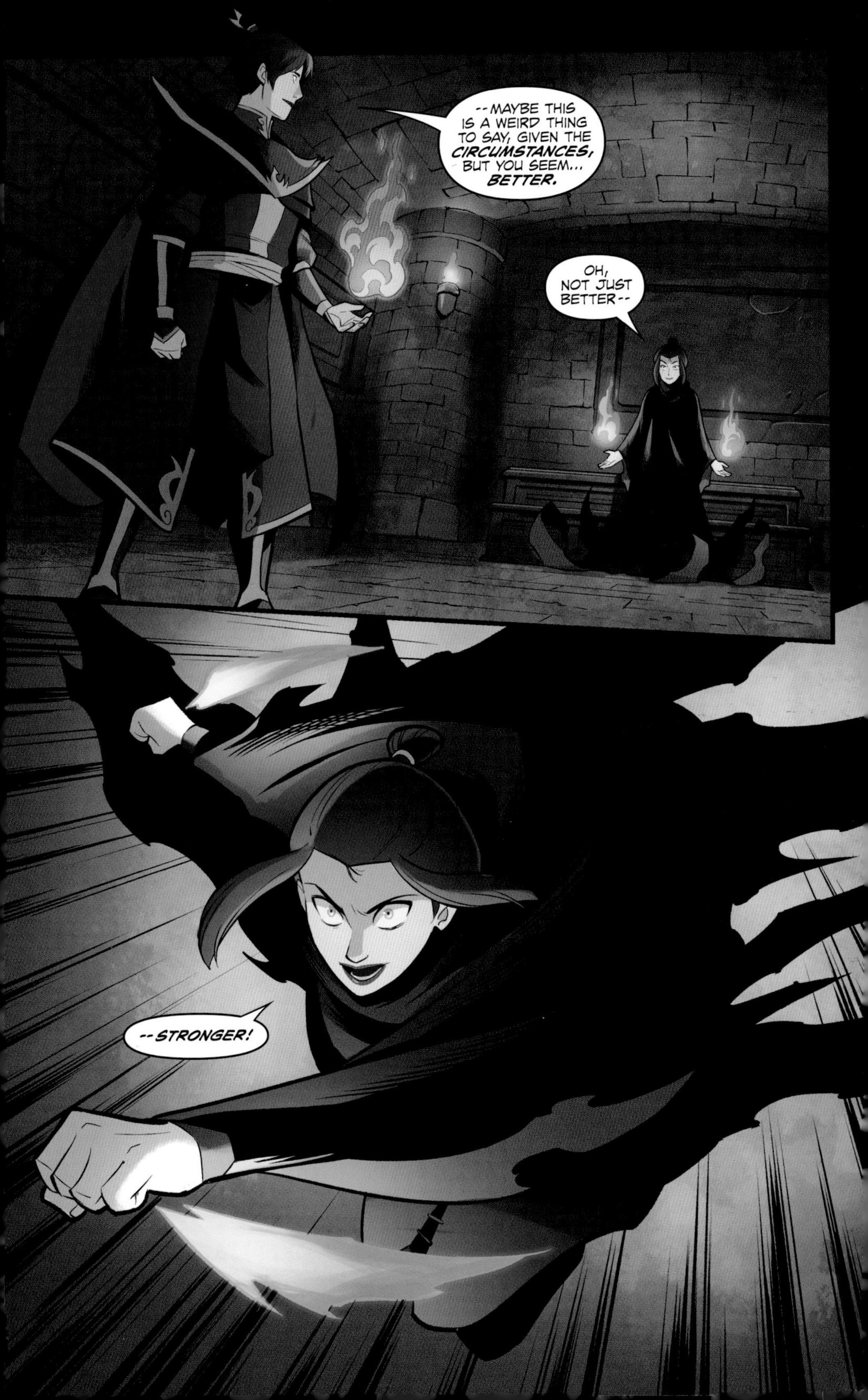
--MAYBE THIS IS A WEIRD THING TO SAY, GIVEN THE *CIRCUMSTANCES,* BUT YOU SEEM... ***BETTER.***
OH, NOT JUST BETTER--
--*STRONGER!*

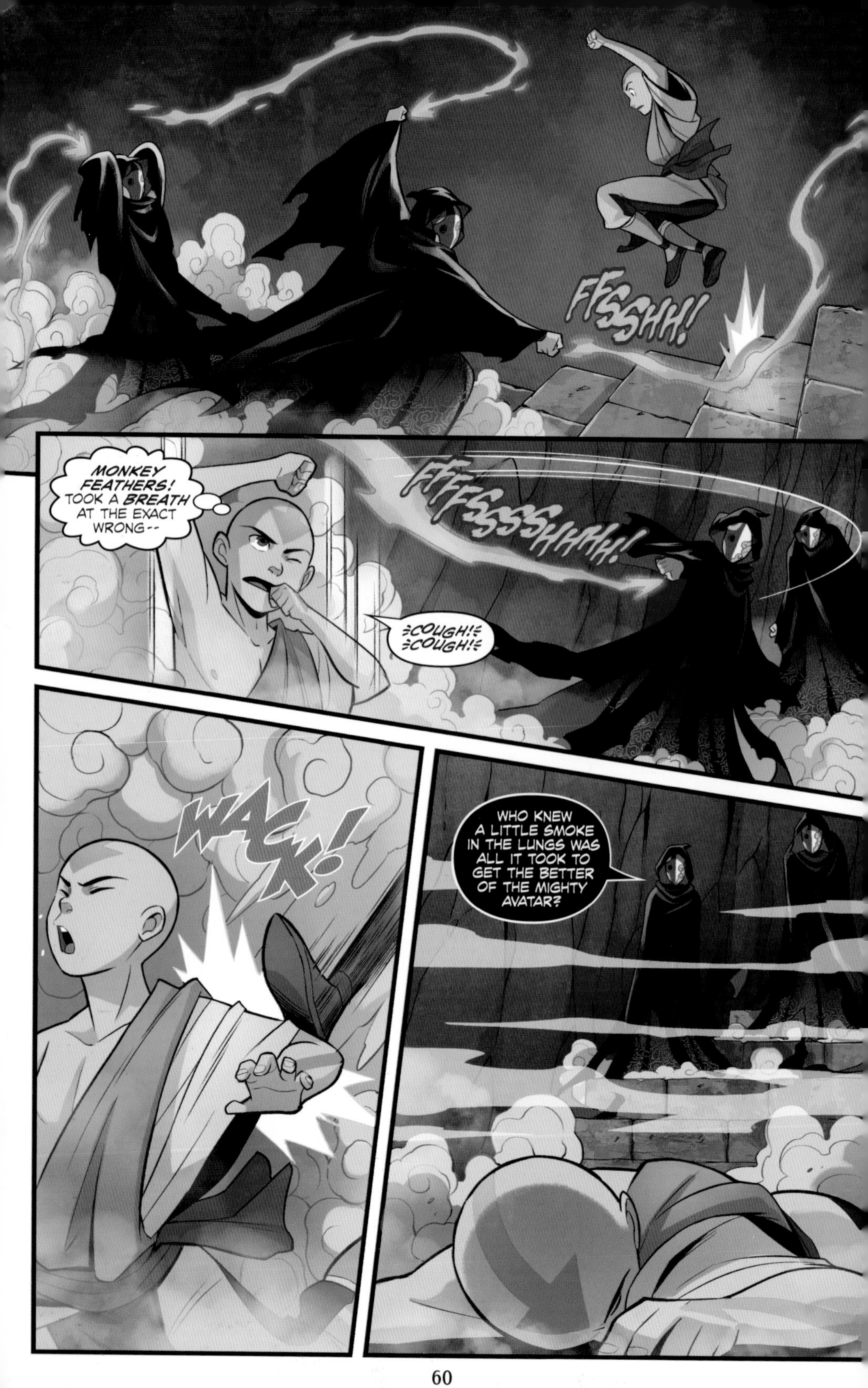

FFSSHH!
MONKEY FEATHERS! TOOK A BREATH AT THE EXACT WRONG--
FFFFSSSSHHHH!
COUGH! COUGH!
WACK!
WHO KNEW A LITTLE SMOKE IN THE LUNGS WAS ALL IT TOOK TO GET THE BETTER OF THE MIGHTY AVATAR?

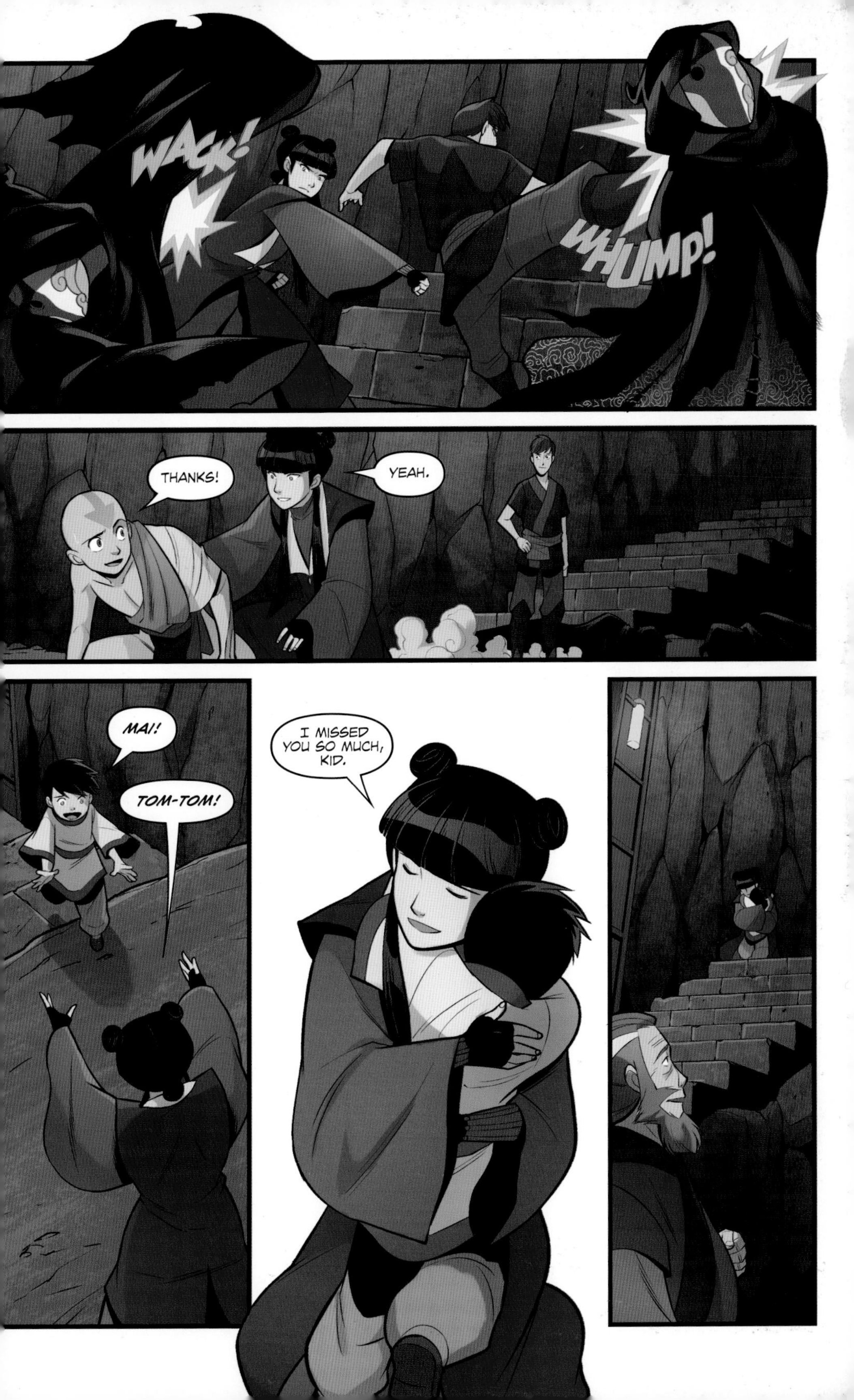

WACK!
WHUMP!
THANKS!
YEAH.
MAI!
TOM-TOM!
I MISSED YOU SO MUCH, KID.

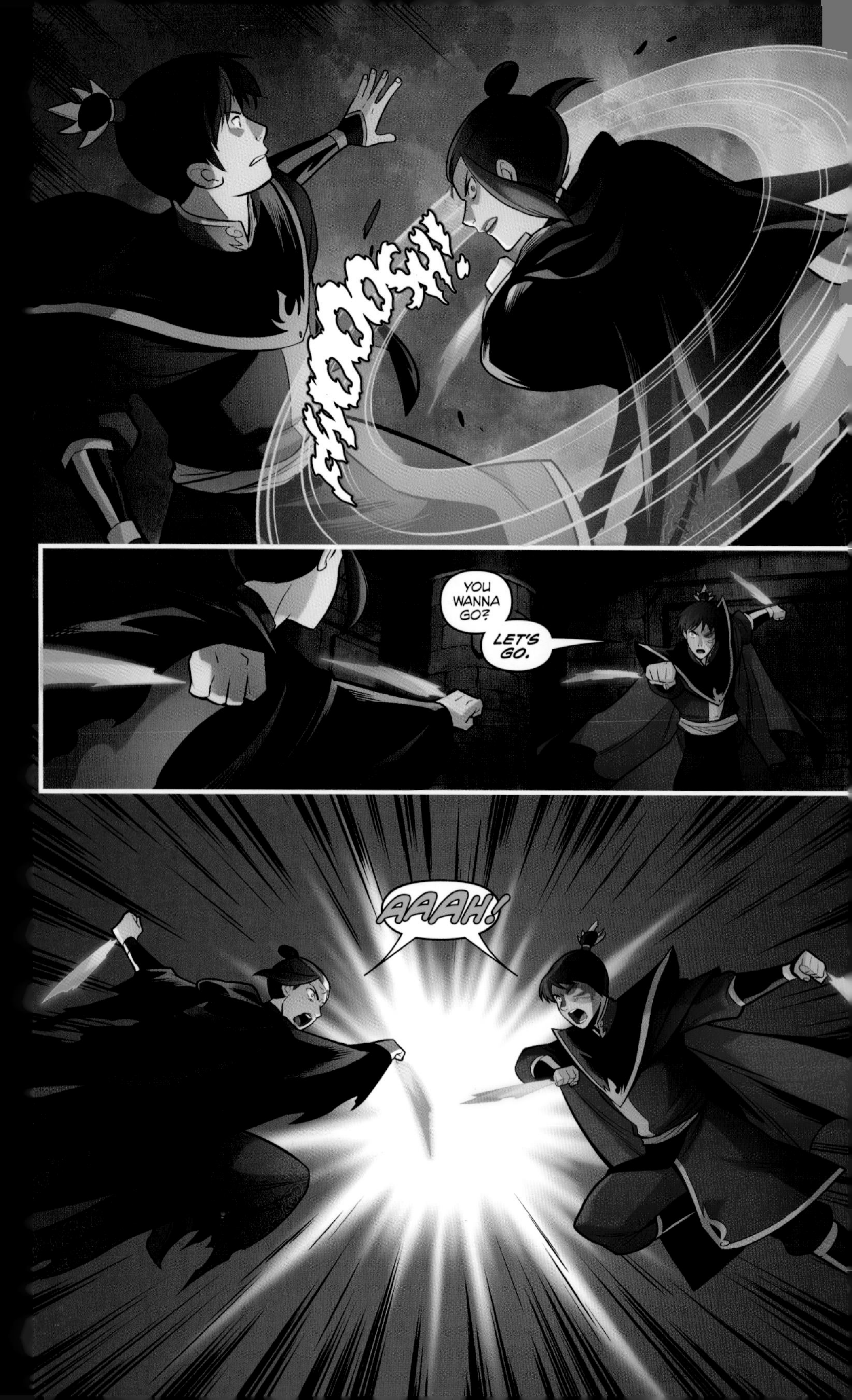
WOOSH!
YOU WANNA GO?
LET'S GO.
AAAH!

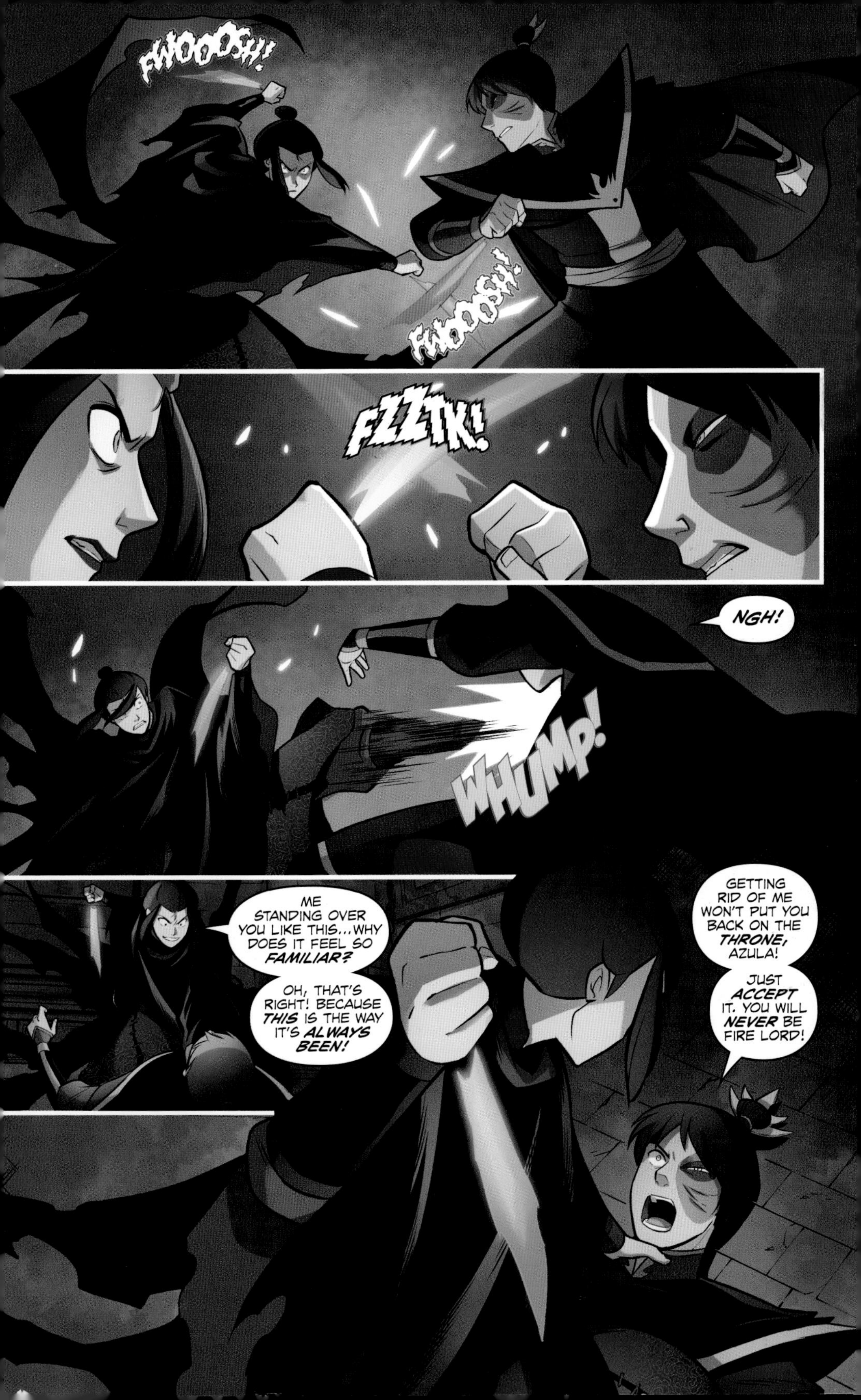
FWOOOSH!
FWOOSH!
FZZZTK!
NGH!
WHUMP!
ME STANDING OVER YOU LIKE THIS...WHY DOES IT FEEL SO FAMILIAR?
OH, THAT'S RIGHT! BECAUSE THIS IS THE WAY IT'S ALWAYS BEEN!
GETTING RID OF ME WON'T PUT YOU BACK ON THE THRONE, AZULA!
JUST ACCEPT IT. YOU WILL NEVER BE FIRE LORD!

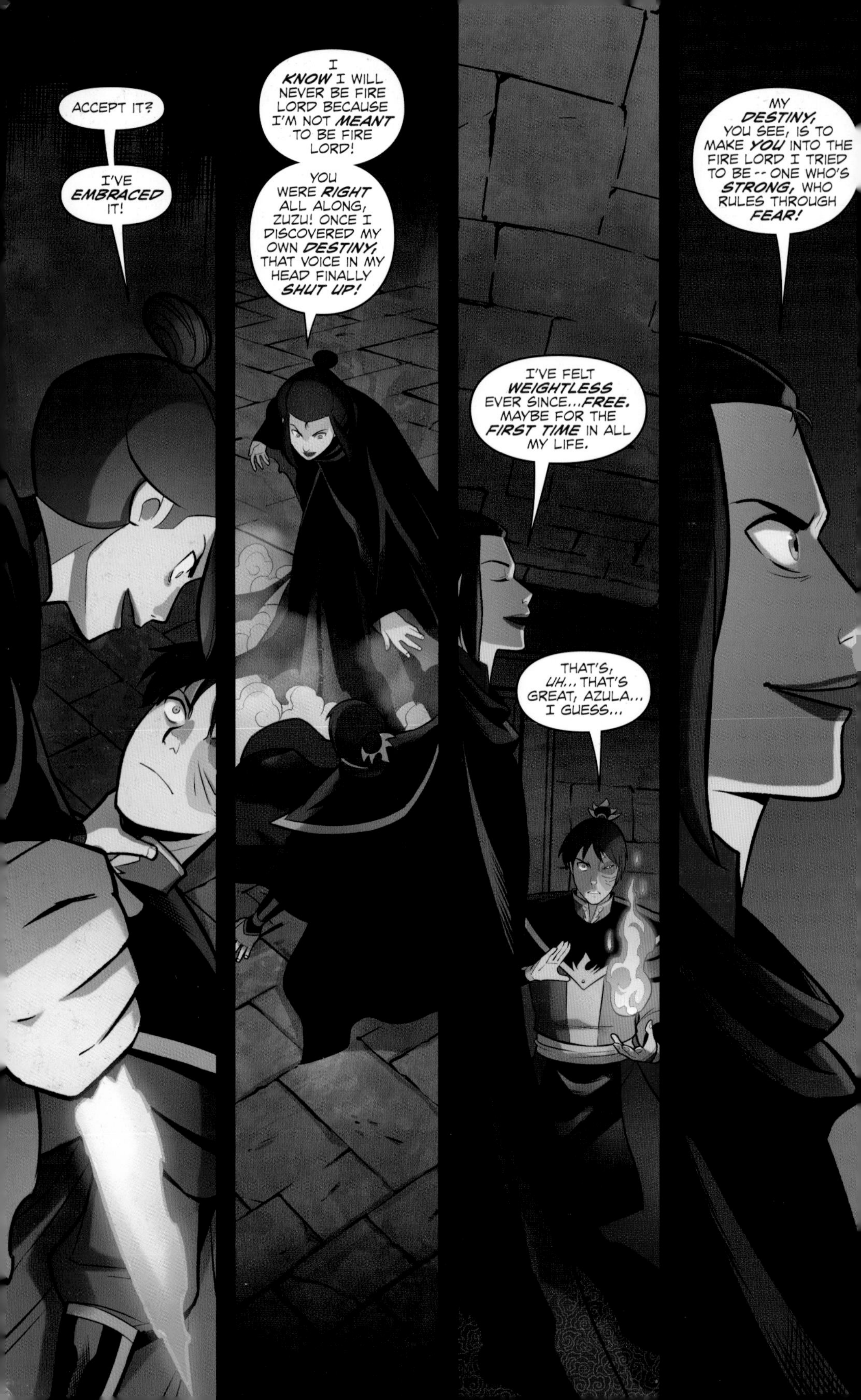

ACCEPT IT?
I'VE EMBRACED IT!
I KNOW I WILL NEVER BE FIRE LORD BECAUSE I'M NOT MEANT TO BE FIRE LORD!
YOU WERE RIGHT ALL ALONG, ZUZU! ONCE I DISCOVERED MY OWN DESTINY, THAT VOICE IN MY HEAD FINALLY SHUT UP!
I'VE FELT WEIGHTLESS EVER SINCE...FREE. MAYBE FOR THE FIRST TIME IN ALL MY LIFE.
THAT'S, UH... THAT'S GREAT, AZULA... I GUESS...
MY DESTINY, YOU SEE, IS TO MAKE YOU INTO THE FIRE LORD I TRIED TO BE -- ONE WHO'S STRONG, WHO RULES THROUGH FEAR!

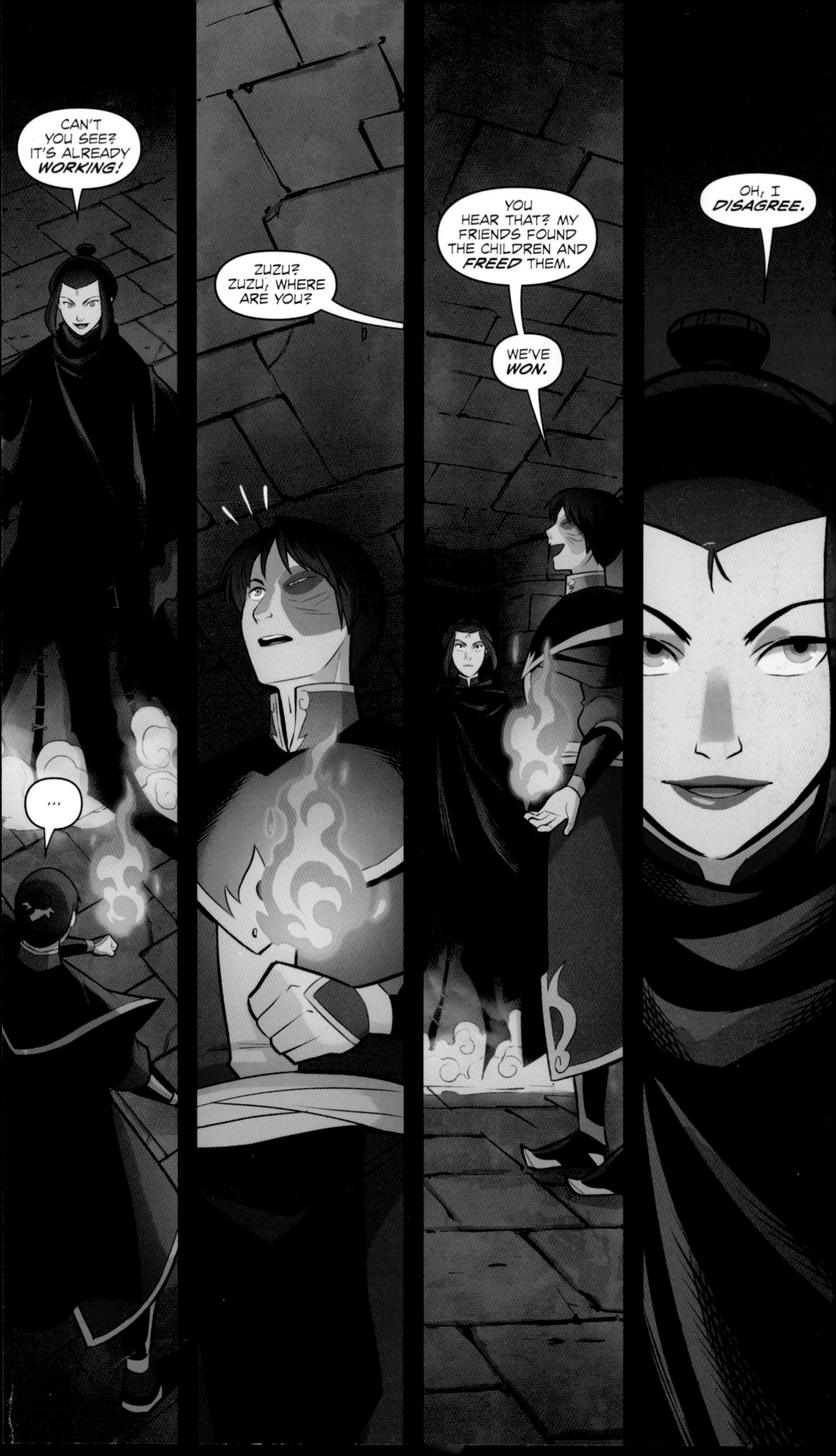
CAN'T YOU SEE? IT'S ALREADY WORKING!
...
ZUZU? ZUZU, WHERE ARE YOU?
YOU HEAR THAT? MY FRIENDS FOUND THE CHILDREN AND FREED THEM.
WE'VE WON.
OH, I DISAGREE.

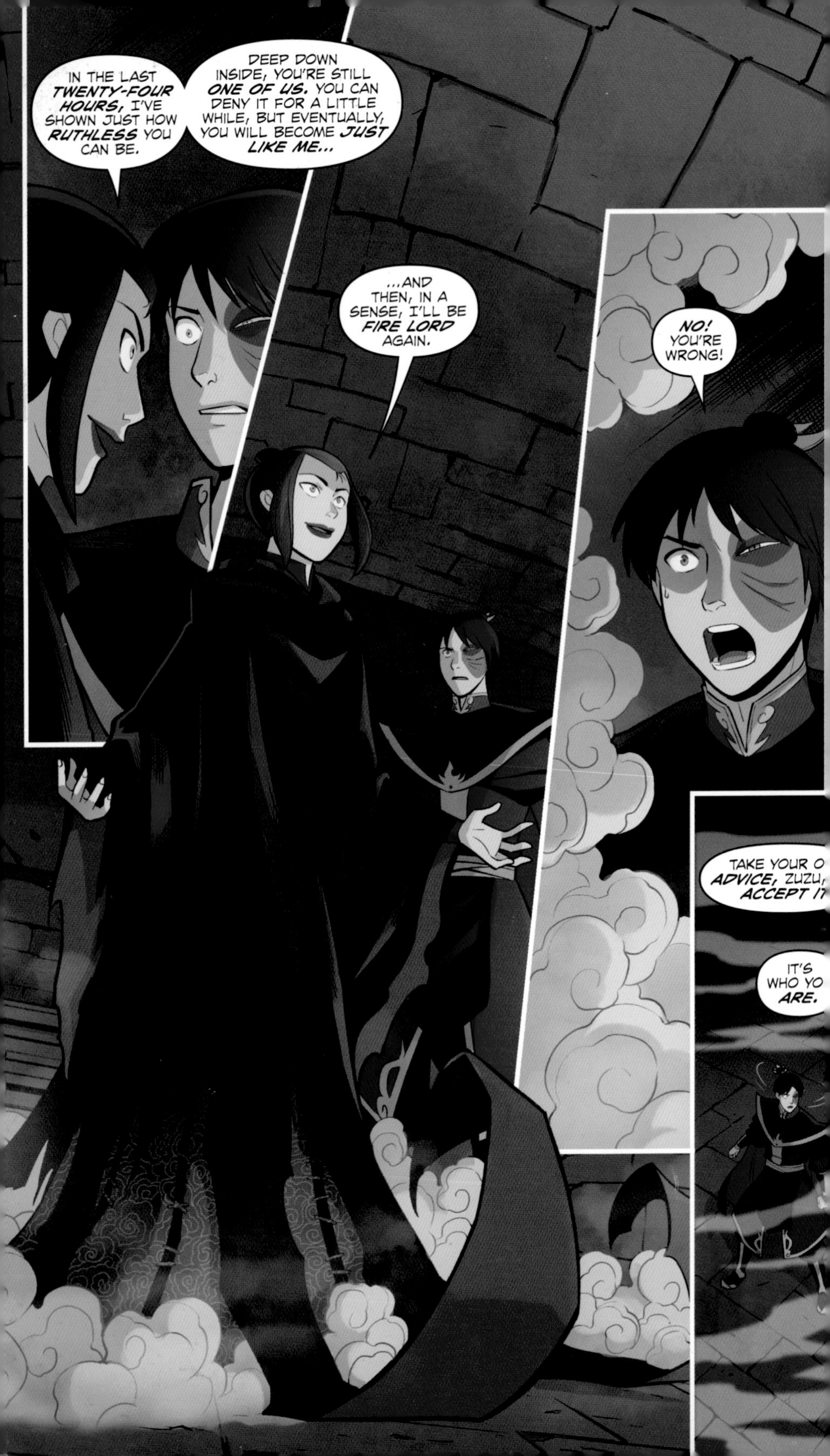
IN THE LAST TWENTY-FOUR HOURS, I'VE SHOWN JUST HOW RUTHLESS YOU CAN BE.
DEEP DOWN INSIDE, YOU'RE STILL ONE OF US. YOU CAN DENY IT FOR A LITTLE WHILE, BUT EVENTUALLY, YOU WILL BECOME JUST LIKE ME...
...AND THEN, IN A SENSE, I'LL BE FIRE LORD AGAIN.
NO! YOU'RE WRONG!
TAKE YOUR O ADVICE, ZUZU, ACCEPT IT
IT'S WHO YO ARE.

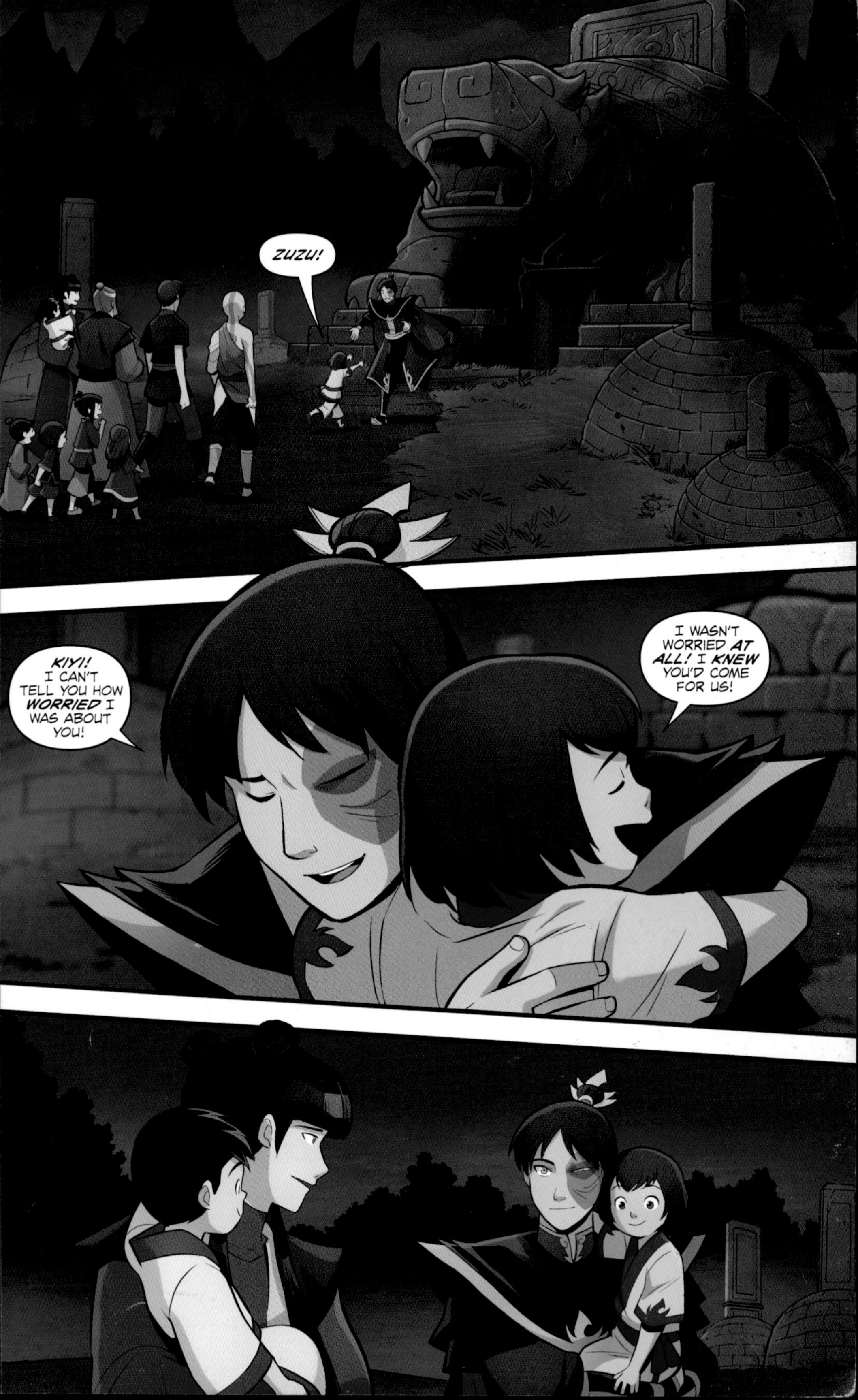
ZUZU!
KIYI! I CAN'T TELL YOU HOW WORRIED I WAS ABOUT YOU!
I WASN'T WORRIED AT ALL! I KNEW YOU'D COME FOR US!

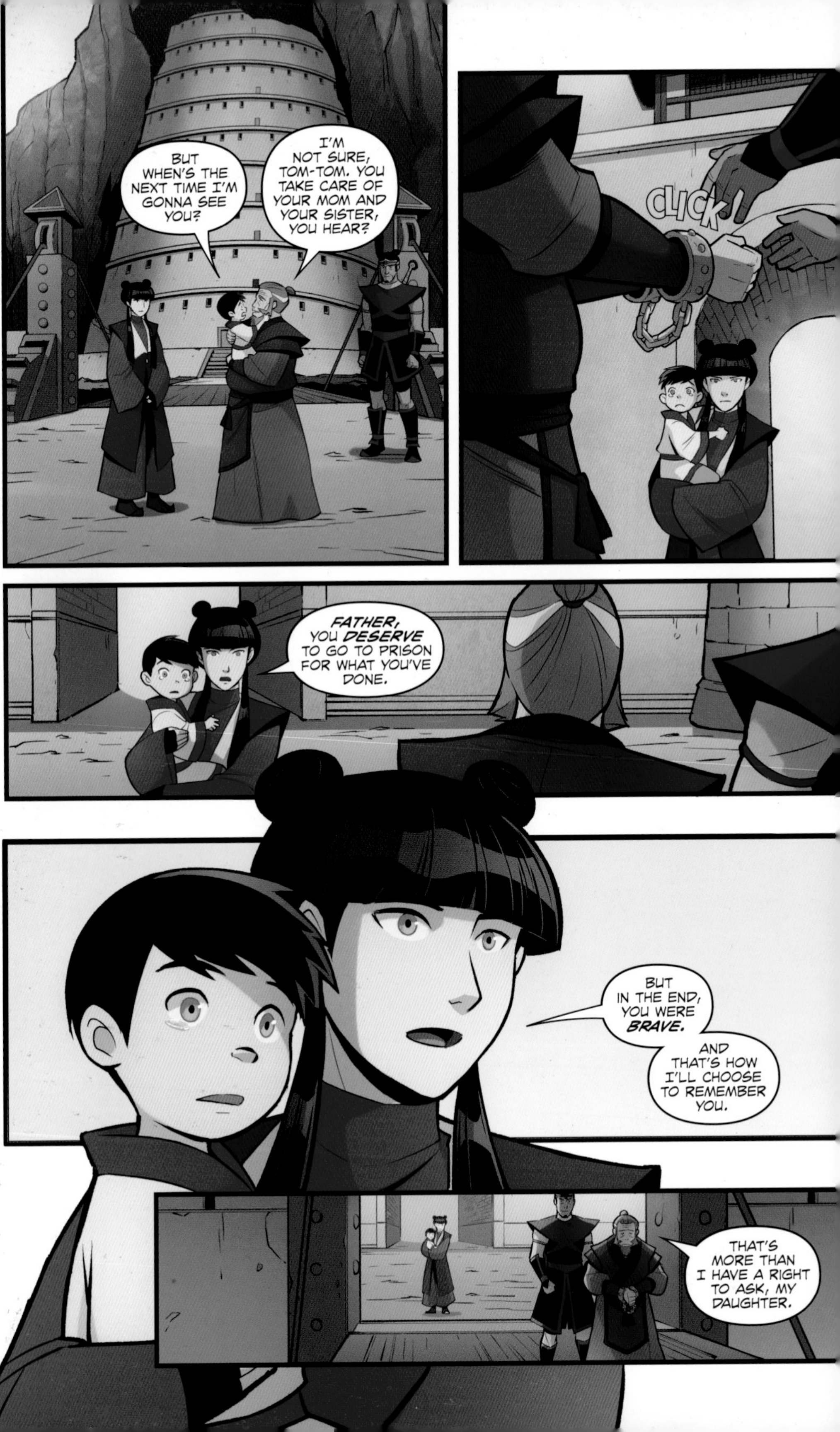
BUT WHEN'S THE NEXT TIME I'M GONNA SEE YOU?
I'M NOT SURE, TOM-TOM. YOU TAKE CARE OF YOUR MOM AND YOUR SISTER, YOU HEAR?
CLICK!
FATHER, YOU DESERVE TO GO TO PRISON FOR WHAT YOU'VE DONE.
BUT IN THE END, YOU WERE BRAVE.
AND THAT'S HOW I'LL CHOOSE TO REMEMBER YOU.
THAT'S MORE THAN I HAVE A RIGHT TO ASK, MY DAUGHTER.

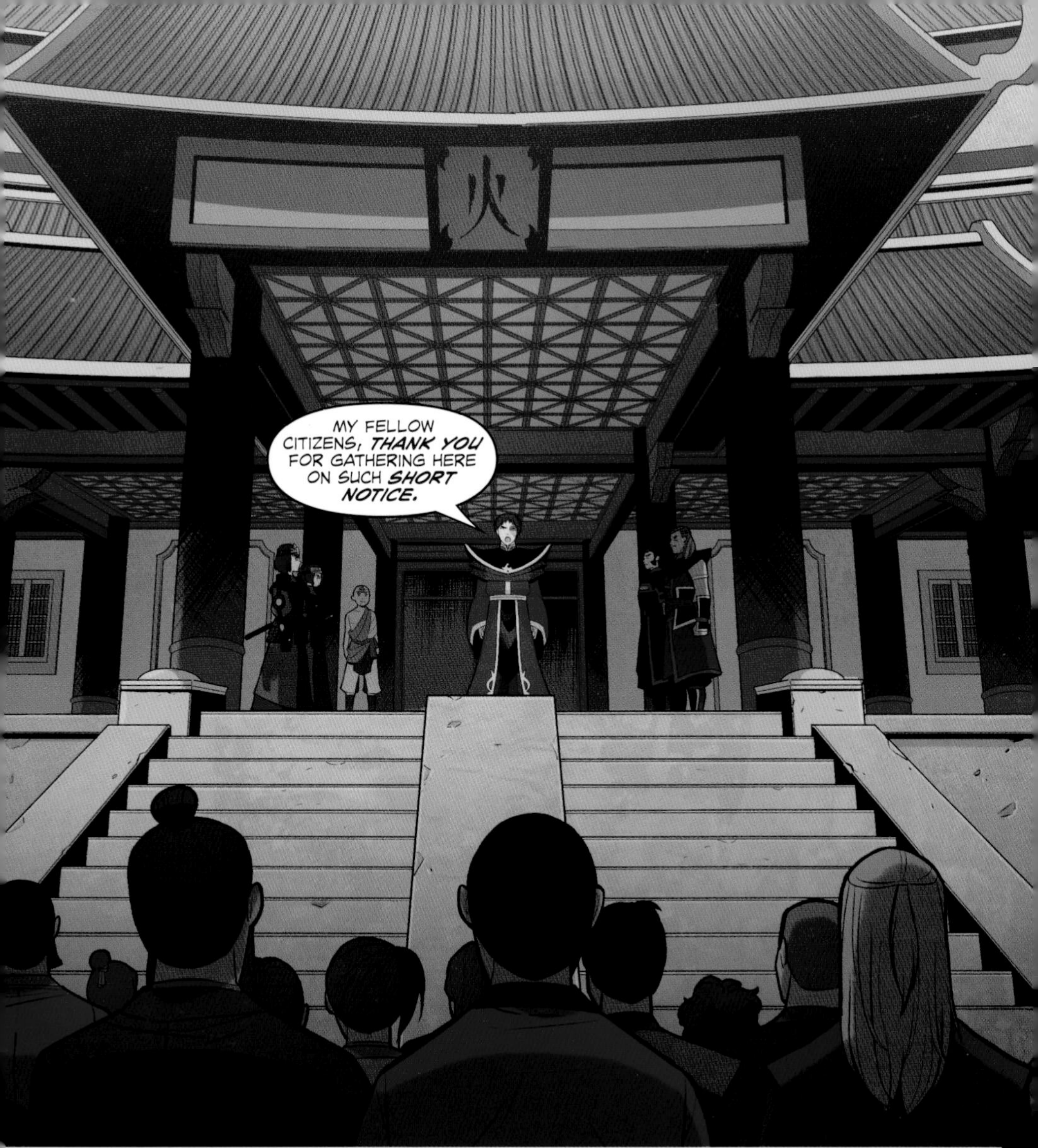
MY FELLOW CITIZENS, THANK YOU FOR GATHERING HERE ON SUCH SHORT NOTICE.

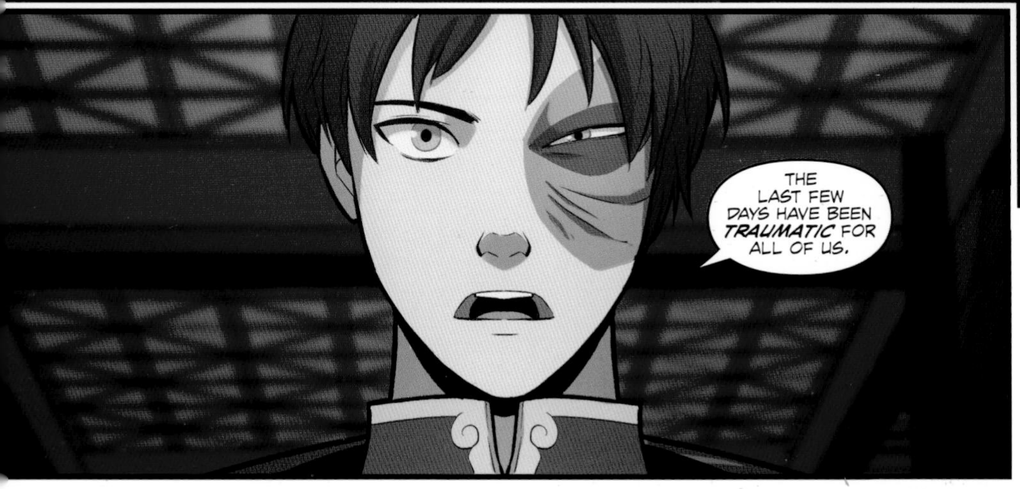
THE LAST FEW DAYS HAVE BEEN TRAUMATIC FOR ALL OF US.

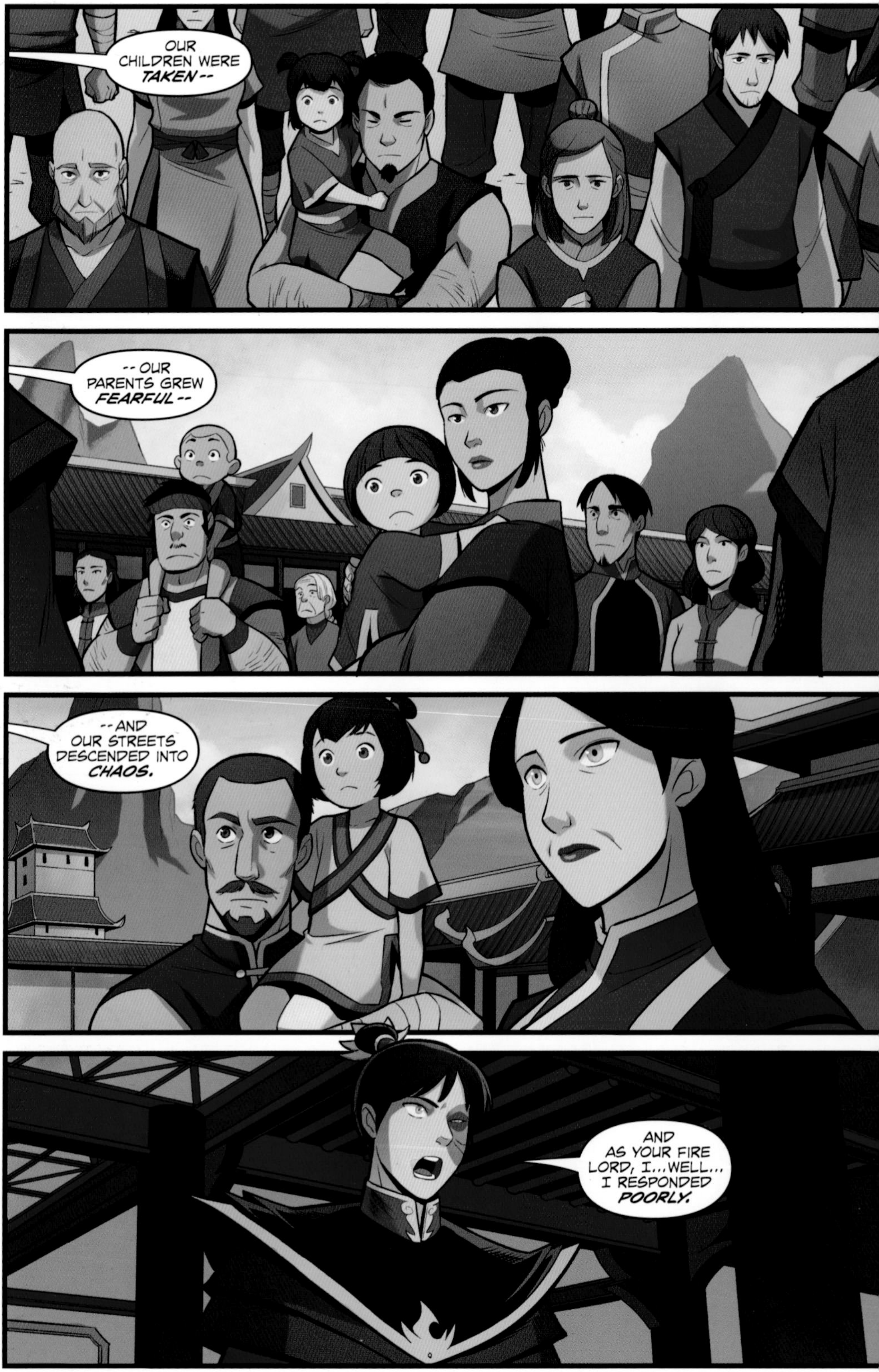
OUR CHILDREN WERE TAKEN--
--OUR PARENTS GREW FEARFUL--
--AND OUR STREETS DESCENDED INTO CHAOS.
AND AS YOUR FIRE LORD, I...WELL... I RESPONDED POORLY.

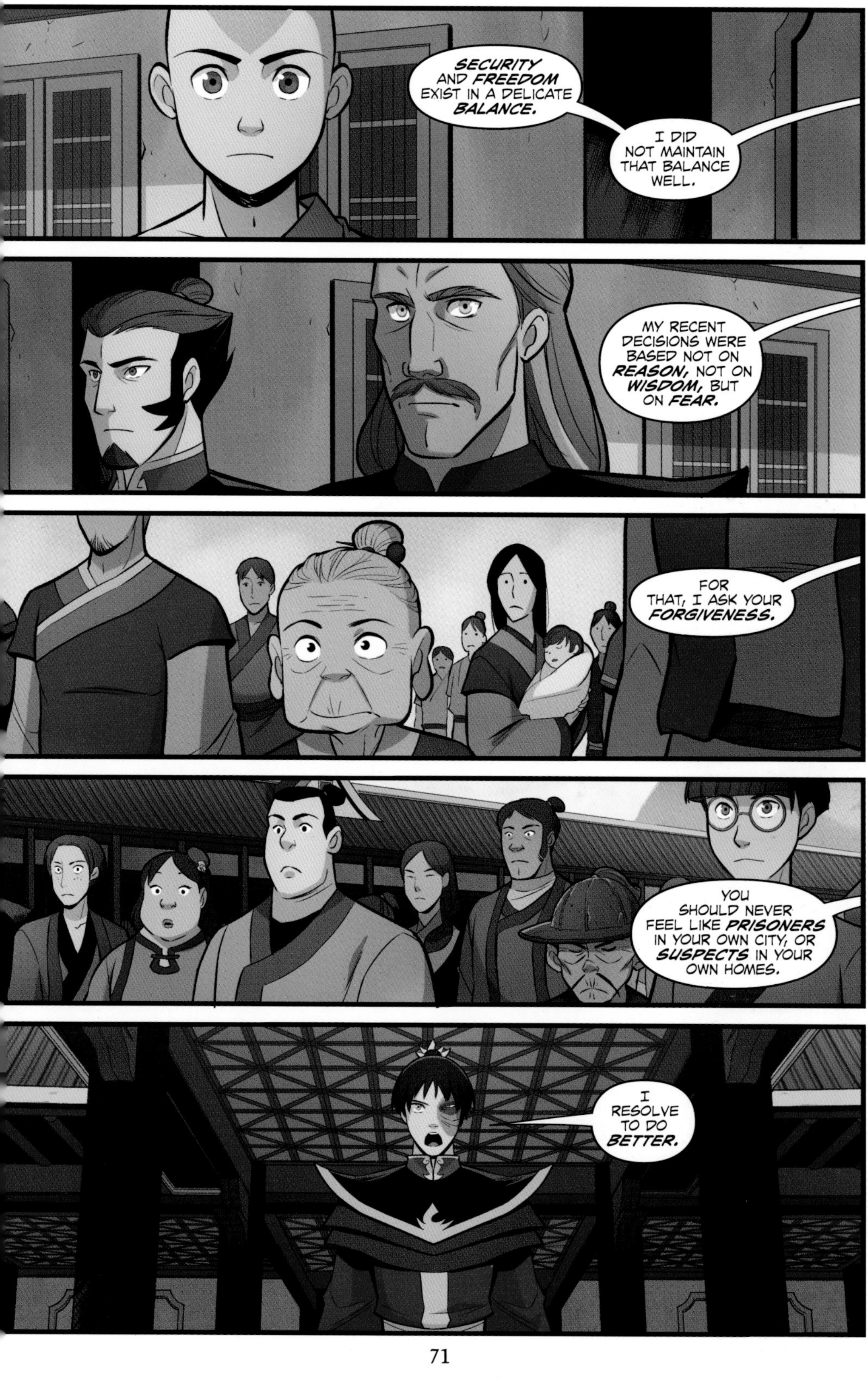
SECURITY AND FREEDOM EXIST IN A DELICATE BALANCE.
I DID NOT MAINTAIN THAT BALANCE WELL.
MY RECENT DECISIONS WERE BASED NOT ON REASON, NOT ON WISDOM, BUT ON FEAR.
FOR THAT, I ASK YOUR FORGIVENESS.
YOU SHOULD NEVER FEEL LIKE PRISONERS IN YOUR OWN CITY, OR SUSPECTS IN YOUR OWN HOMES.
I RESOLVE TO DO BETTER.

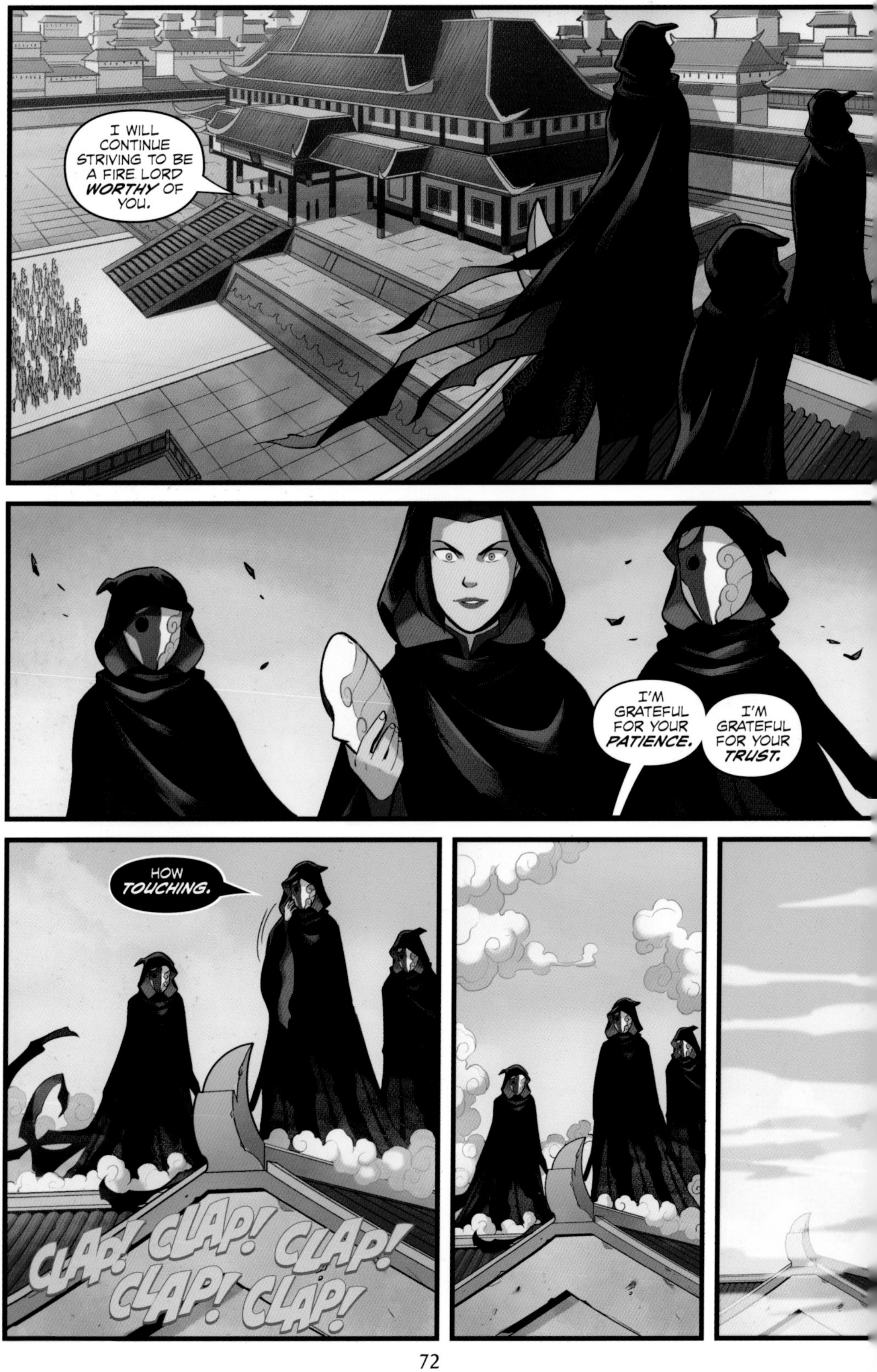
I WILL CONTINUE STRIVING TO BE A FIRE LORD WORTHY OF YOU.
I'M GRATEFUL FOR YOUR PATIENCE.
I'M GRATEFUL FOR YOUR TRUST.
HOW TOUCHING.
CLAP! CLAP! CLAP! CLAP! CLAP!

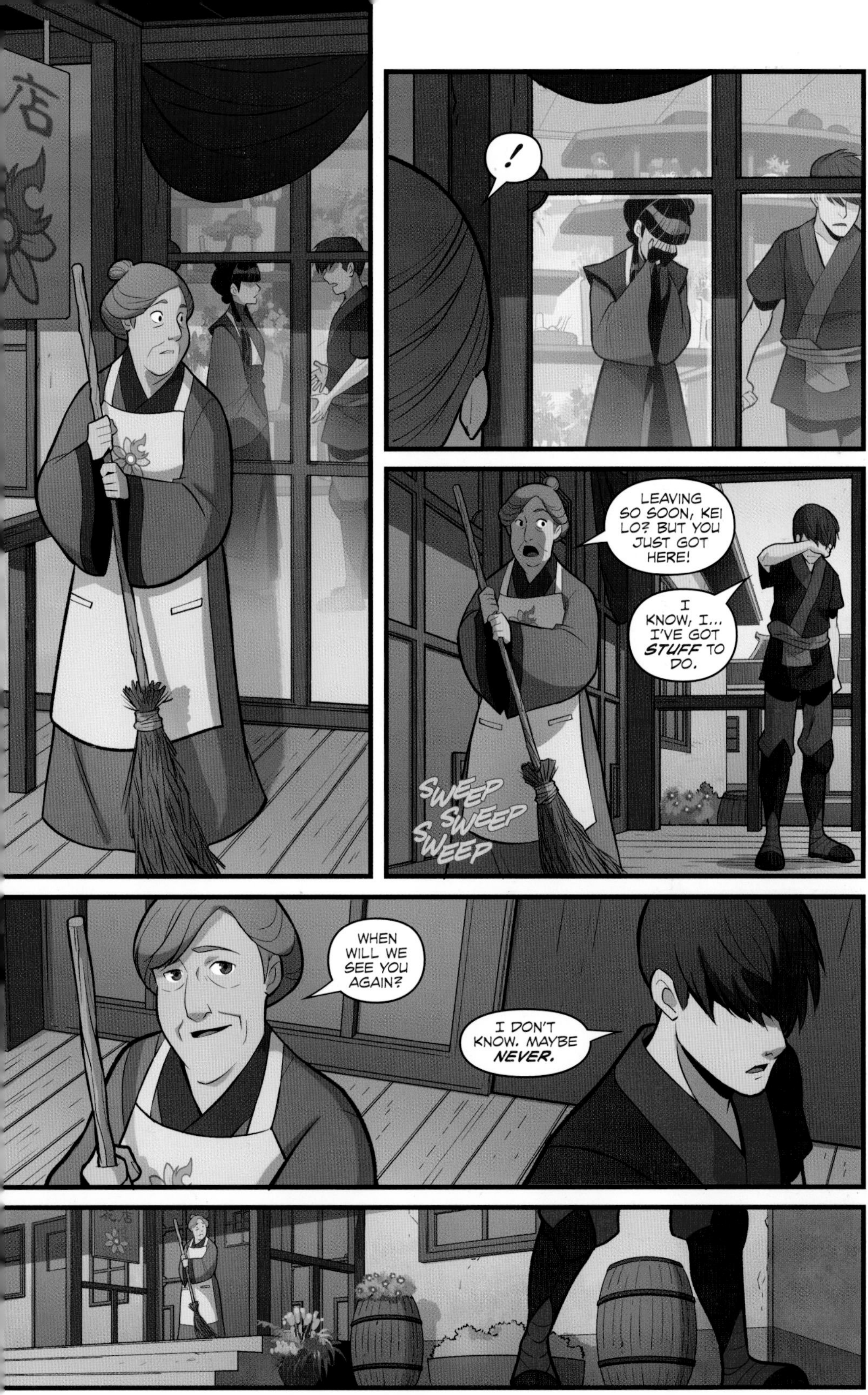
!
LEAVING SO SOON, KEI LO? BUT YOU JUST GOT HERE!
I KNOW, I... I'VE GOT STUFF TO DO.
SWEEP SWEEP SWEEP
WHEN WILL WE SEE YOU AGAIN?
I DON'T KNOW. MAYBE NEVER.

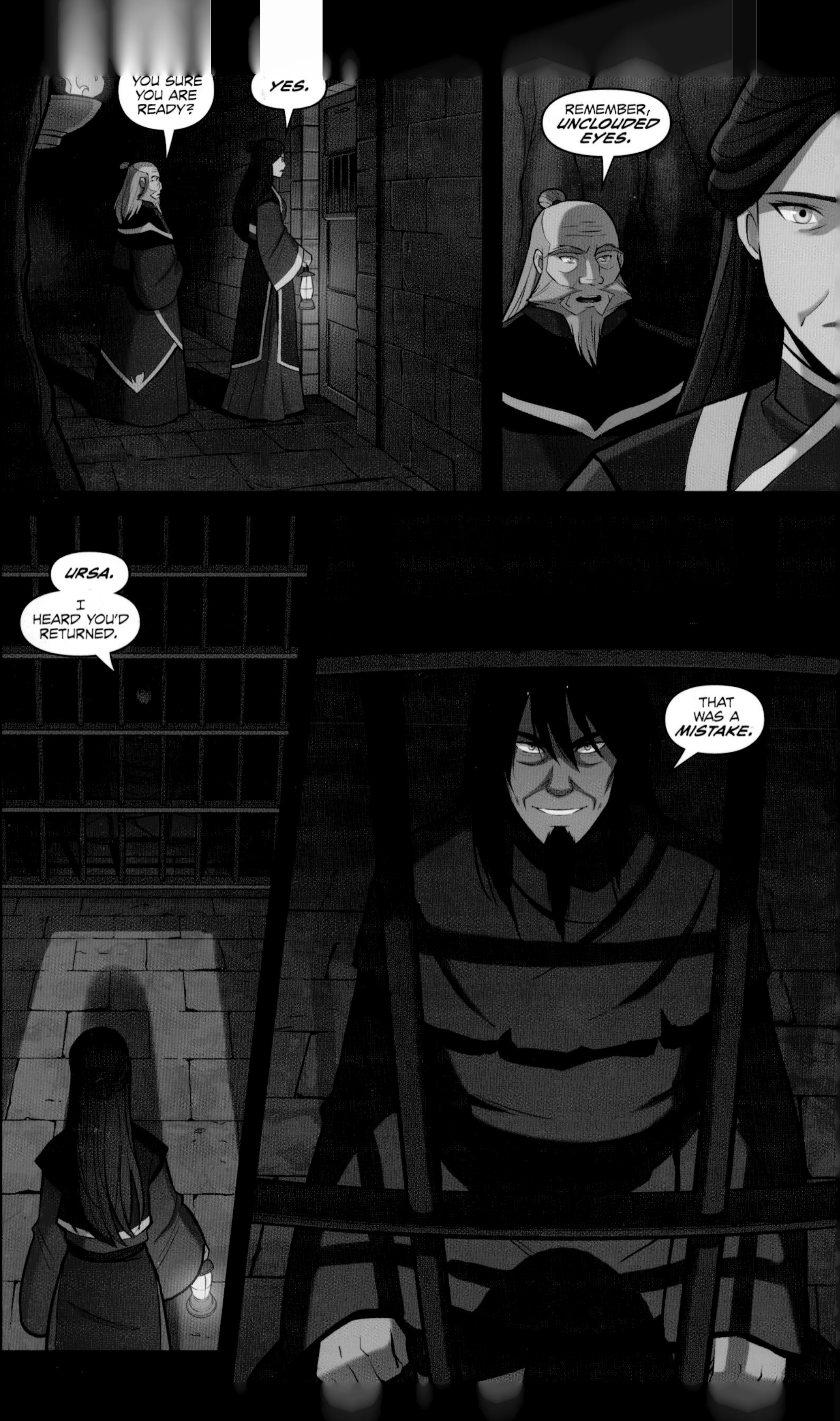
YOU SURE YOU ARE READY?
YES.
REMEMBER, UNCLOUDED EYES.
URSA.
I HEARD YOU'D RETURNED.
THAT WAS A MISTAKE.

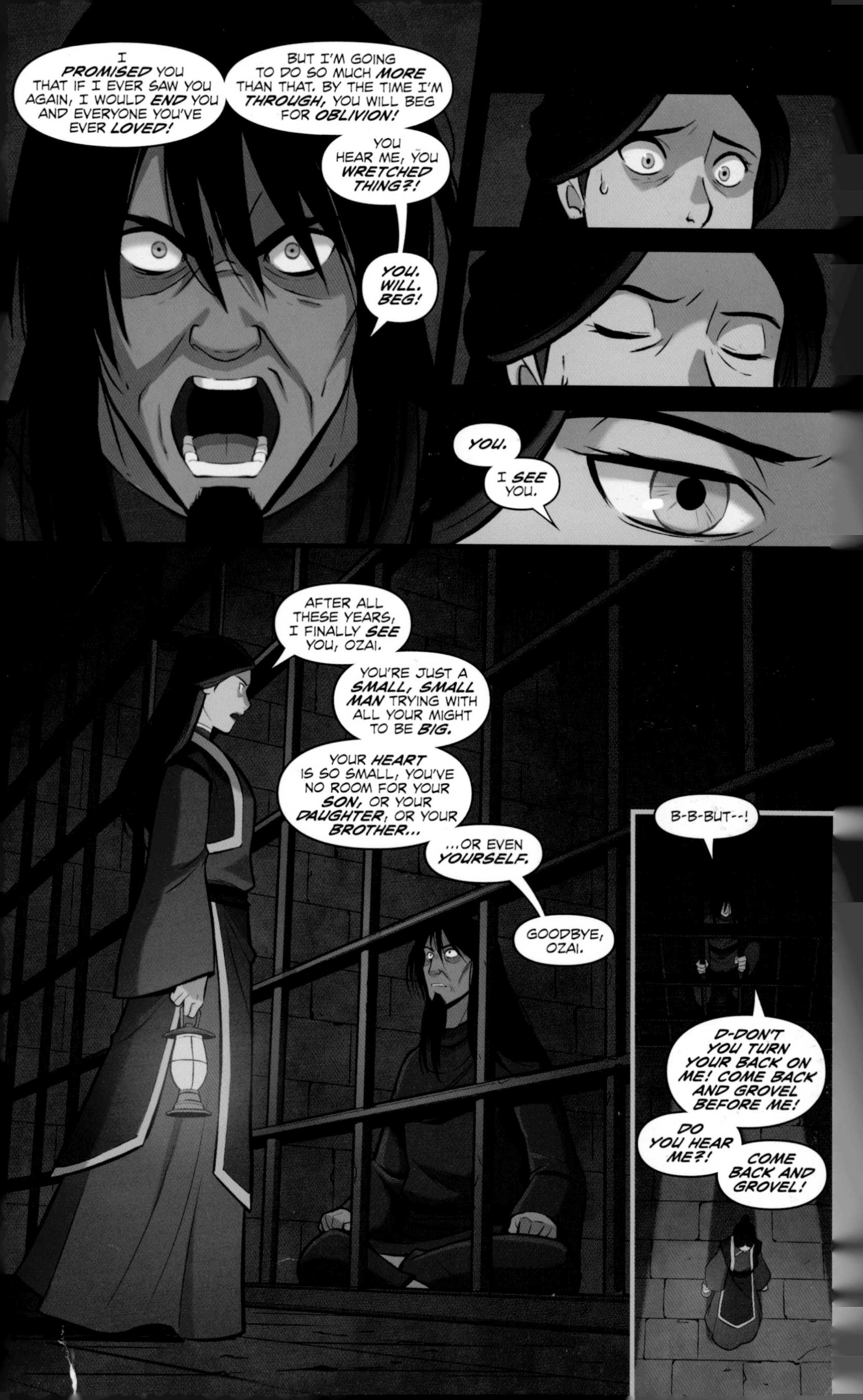
I PROMISED YOU THAT IF I EVER SAW YOU AGAIN, I WOULD END YOU AND EVERYONE YOU'VE EVER LOVED!
BUT I'M GOING TO DO SO MUCH MORE THAN THAT. BY THE TIME I'M THROUGH, YOU WILL BEG FOR OBLIVION!
YOU HEAR ME, YOU WRETCHED THING?!
YOU. WILL. BEG!
YOU.
I SEE YOU.
AFTER ALL THESE YEARS, I FINALLY SEE YOU, OZAI.
YOU'RE JUST A SMALL, SMALL MAN TRYING WITH ALL YOUR MIGHT TO BE BIG.
YOUR HEART IS SO SMALL, YOU'VE NO ROOM FOR YOUR SON, OR YOUR DAUGHTER, OR YOUR BROTHER...
...OR EVEN YOURSELF.
GOODBYE, OZAI.
B-B-BUT--!
D-DON'T YOU TURN YOUR BACK ON ME! COME BACK AND GROVEL BEFORE ME!
DO YOU HEAR ME?!
COME BACK AND GROVEL!

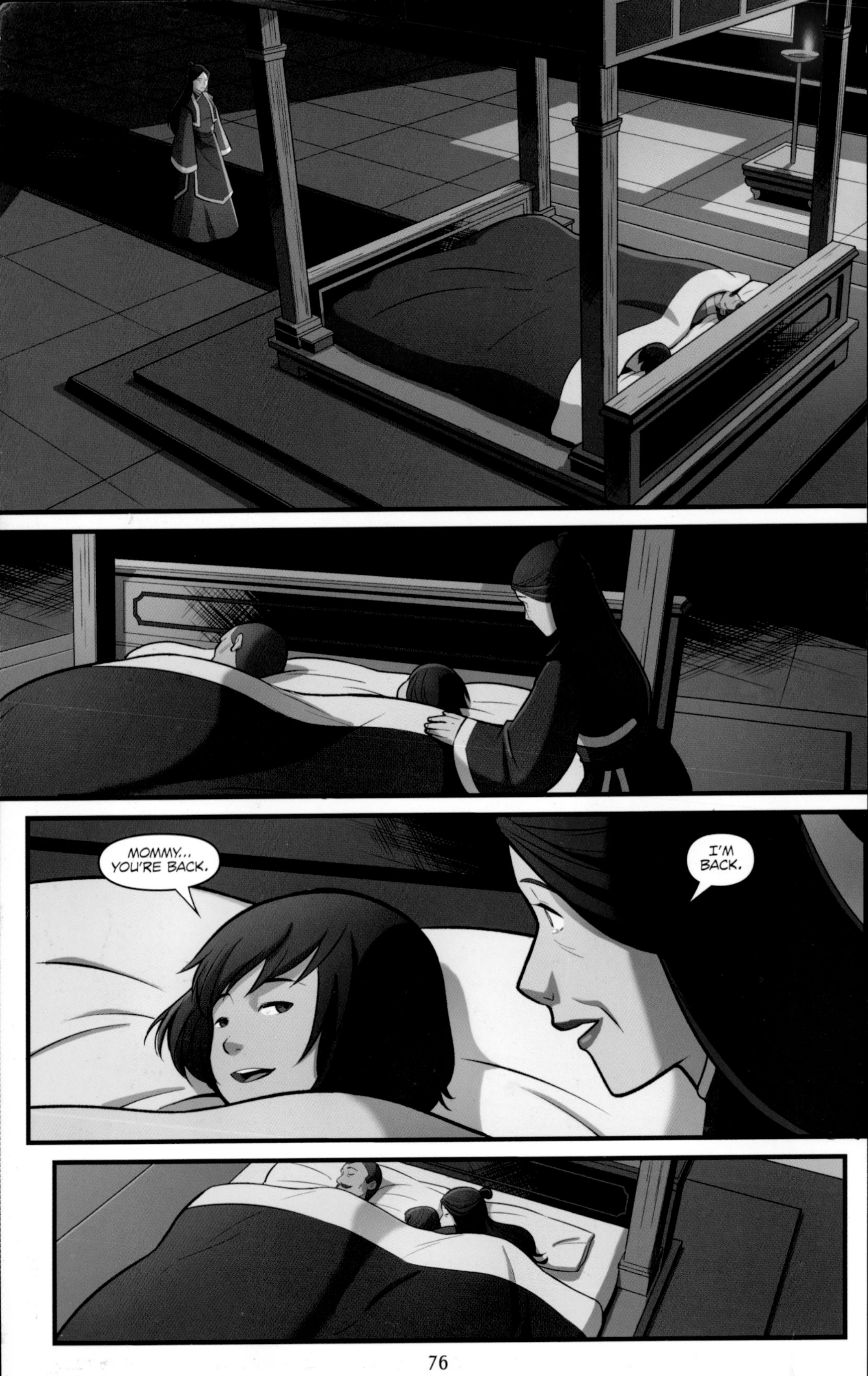
MOMMY... YOU'RE BACK.
I'M BACK.

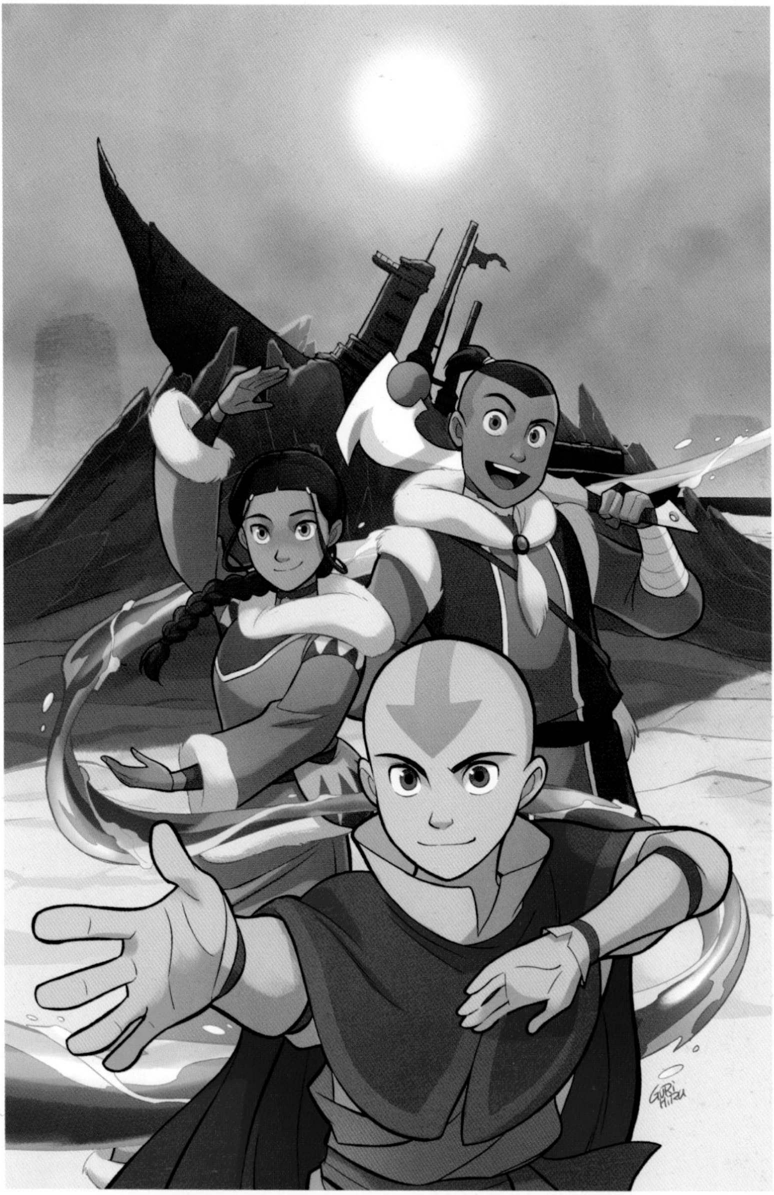

COMING IN OCTOBER 2016

Katara and Sokka return to the Southern Water Tribe in . . .

NORTH AND SOUTH • PART ONE

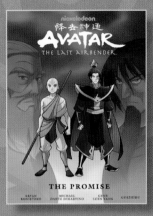

nickelodeon
降去神通
AVATAR
THE LAST AIRBENDER
THE PROMISE
BRYAN KONIETZKO
MICHAEL DANTE DIMARTINO
GENE LUEN YANG
GURIHIRU

nickelodeon
降去神通
AVATAR
THE LAST AIRBENDER
THE PROMISE · PART THREE

Avatar: The Last Airbender—The Promise Library Edition
978-1-61655-074-5 $39.99

Avatar: The Last Airbender—The Promise Part 1
978-1-59582-811-8 $10.99

Avatar: The Last Airbender—The Promise Part 2
978-1-59582-875-0 $10.99

Avatar: The Last Airbender—The Promise Part 3
978-1-59582-941-2 $10.99

降去神通
AVATAR
THE LAST AIRBENDER
THE SEARCH
BRYAN KONIETZKO
MICHAEL DANTE DiMARTINO
GENE LUEN YANG
GURIHIRU

nickelodeon
降去神通
AVATAR
THE SEARCH · PART ONE
THE SEARCH · PART THREE

Avatar: The Last Airbender—The Search Library Edition
978-1-61655-226-8 $39.99

Avatar: The Last Airbender—The Search Part 1
978-1-61655-054-7 $10.99

Avatar: The Last Airbender—The Search Part 2
978-1-61655-190-2 $10.99

Avatar: The Last Airbender—The Search Part 3
978-1-61655-184-1 $10.99

nickelodeon
降去神通
AVATAR
THE LAST AIRBENDER
THE LOST ADVENTURES

Avatar: The Last Airbender—The Art of the Animated Series
978-1-59582-504-9 $34.99

Avatar: The Last Airbender—The Lost Adventures
978-1-59582-748-7 $14.99

AVAILABLE AT YOUR LOCAL COMICS SHOP OR BOOKSTORE.
To find a comics shop in your area, call 1-888-266-4226
For more information or to order direct, visit DarkHorse.com or call 1-800-862-0052

GO BEHIND-THE-SCENES of the follow-up to the smash-hit series *Avatar: the Last Airbender*! Each volume features hundreds of pieces of never-before-seen artwork created during the development of *The Legend of Korra*. With captions from creators Michael Dante DiMartino and Bryan Konietzko throughout, this is an intimate look inside the creative process that brought the mystical world of bending and a new generation of heroes to life!

nickelodeon

THE LEGEND OF KORRA

THE ART OF THE ANIMATED SERIES

BOOK ONE: AIR
978-1-61655-168-1 | $34.99

BOOK TWO: SPIRITS
978-1-61655-462-0 | $34.99

BOOK THREE: CHANGE
978-1-61655-565-8 | $34.99

BOOK FOUR: BALANCE
978-1-61655-687-7 | $34.99